Genesis Ideology

GENESIS IDEOLOGY

Essays on the
Uses and Meanings
of Stories

David H. Aaron

CASCADE *Books* · Eugene, Oregon

GENESIS IDEOLOGY
Essays on the Uses and Meanings of Stories

Cascade Books
An Imprint of Wipf and Stock Publishers
199 W. 8th Ave., Suite 3
Eugene, OR 97401

www.wipfandstock.com

PAPERBACK ISBN: 978-1-5326-0945-9
HARDCOVER ISBN: 978-1-5326-0947-3
EBOOK ISBN: 978-1-5326-0946-6

Cataloguing-in-Publication data:

Names: Aaron, David H., 1956–, author.
Title: Genesis ideology : essays on the uses and meanings of stories / David H. Aaron.
Description: Eugene, OR: Cascade Books, 2017.
Identifiers: ISBN 978-1-5326-0945-9 (paperback) | ISBN 978-1-5326-0947-3 (hardcover) | ISBN 978-1-5326-0946-6 (ebook).
Subjects: LCSH: Bible. O.T. Genesis—Criticism, interpretation, etc.
Classification: BS1235 A27 2017 (print) | BS1235 (ebook).

Manufactured in the U.S.A.   SEPTEMBER 25, 2017

For Marianne and Ronald Aaron

Proverbs 23:25

Contents

Preface

There are many conventions for representing the Hebrew names of God in English translations. I will explain here what the reader can expect in this book.

In some contexts, I have used the transliteration "Yahweh" for the four Hebrew consonants, *Y-H-W-H*, commonly known as Israel's God's name. This long-standing practice originated among nineteenth-century German scholars; hence the *w* for the Hebrew letter English readers would represent with *v* (*w* in German sounds like English *v*). It is also possible that the Hebrew letter *v* sounded closer to *w* in antiquity, as is the case in other Semitic languages. I emphasize that this is a convention because, in fact, we do not know how the four-lettered name of Israel's God would have been pronounced in antiquity. Jewish tradition has it that the name's actual sound was lost during the Second Temple Period, when it was ostensibly only pronounced by Priests in the Temple's innermost holy chamber. A pronunciation could be lost because Semitic languages in antiquity were only written with consonants but no vowels.

In other parts of this book, I have used the word "LORD" in small caps. This seemed particularly fitting when the language is formulaic, such as in a blessing or in a standard biblical phrase. This practice originates with the tradition of biblical readings and liturgical recitations in synagogues that supplied the Tetragrammaton with a euphemistic substitute for the actual name of God. Thus, whenever the Tetragrammaton appears in a synagogue context, one says "Adonai," which literally translates to "my Lord." The convention of using small caps signals to the reader that underlying the translation is the divine name, rather than a more casual reference to "lord," which will also appear in passages we will discuss below.

I am grateful for Chris Rohmann's critical eye, which brought about numerous improvements to this manuscript.

In most of the essays that follow, a cluster of Genesis chapters provides the core themes to be investigated. Where appropriate, the relevant chapters are indicated after the title. Readers unfamiliar with these chapters are encouraged to read them prior to reading any given essay. That is, the essays assume a base knowledge of the story line. Translations of the original Hebrew offered in these essays are my own. Consequently, they will not overlap completely with published translations. Biblical references follow the *Chicago Manual of Style*.

Introduction: The Book of Genesis

The book of Genesis is the first book of the Torah's five, known in Hebrew—as were all books in antiquity—by its first significant word or phrase: *B'rāsheyt*. Of course, the very notion of a "book" in antiquity was quite different from what we associate with that word today. Anything that occupied a scroll was called *a book*. A collection of materials that barely amounted to more than a few pages in today's formats would still be called a book if it occupied a scroll. Originally, the five books that now constitute the Torah were five separate scrolls. The book of Genesis was recognized as the first book because its subject matter relates to material that is temporally prior to the subject matter of the books that follow, but not because it was the first of the five books to be written. In printed versions of the Hebrew Bible today, the books of the Torah and the historical narratives of Joshua, Judges, Samuel, and Kings, are sequenced on the basis of the stories they tell. We can assume nothing about the date of a passage's composition or the alleged date of an episode recorded in a biblical book. A passage treating an episode ascribed to the sixth century BCE might have been written many years before another passage dealing with an "event" ascribed to the eighth century BCE.

The Torah we now have took its current form after the destruction of the First Temple of Jerusalem—that is, after 586 BCE. Exactly when cannot be established with certainty. Scholars offer a wide array of hypotheses, spanning from the end of the sixth century BCE down into the third century BCE. While many who take religiously conservative approaches to Torah are ready to acknowledge a post-586 *redaction* (thorough editing) of the text, most traditional Jews and Christian still insist that its content— its stories and laws, its characters and ideology—date from the period of the First Temple, in some cases, even deriving from King David's era itself (tenth century BCE). Others remain committed to the notion that the

1

Torah's content stems from the eras reflected in the earliest stories of the Genesis Patriarchs and Moses' own lifetime in Exodus. This would ostensibly situate the sources for these stories as early as the eighteenth century BCE in the case of the Patriarchs, and perhaps the fifteenth century with respect to the stories of the Exodus. Some who advocate for this position fear that if the narratives, or at least the "traditions" contained in the Torah, were not authentic to the eras and personalities it describes, the narratives' status would be diminished. Little can be said by those who believe in this compositional chronology as to how such sources reached us. Usually, scholars and religionists alike attribute their preservation to what is commonly referred to as "oral tradition."

We have no objectively verifiable means for establishing the antiquity of any given *tradition* narrated within the Torah. All we can do is work with the evidence that *suggests* when things were written down. The oldest surviving manuscripts of the Torah, as well as the other biblical books, were found in the region of Qumran by the Dead Sea in Israel (hence, they are called the Dead Sea Scrolls). The oldest biblical materials discovered there date to the second and first centuries BCE. We are quite confident that these are not the original scrolls of the Torah, but copies that were collected and stashed away in a clandestine library to preserve what the collectors feared might otherwise be lost. Indeed, biblical books were not the only texts found at Qumran. There is an array of non-canonical literature, translations, and the writings of sectarian groups. The library itself was probably hidden just prior to the fall of Jerusalem to the Romans in 70 CE. Someone had the foresight to sequester these books so that they would not be lost to history as casualties of war. While some of the non-biblical books found near Qumran did manage to survive in other contexts, many of the writings hidden there only exist today by virtue of having been deposited in those caves.

As far as hard, physical evidence goes, there remains quite a gap between the dates of these oldest manuscripts and when most scholars believe the literature of the Hebrew Bible—and the Torah in particular—was actually written. And then, for some, there is a gap between its presumed date of composition (let's use the fifth century BCE as a more conservative hypothesis for the moment) and its origins. Despite this lack of hard evidence, many insist, as we have noted, that the traditions reflected in the literature were transmitted over the generations in oral form prior to being committed to writing. The argument for oral tradition has become ubiquitous and conventional, appearing unquestioned in college textbooks, adult education courses, and scholarly monographs alike. The insistence on the orality of traditions emerged as part of an attempt to ascribe remote antiquity to something for which there was no conclusive way to date the material. Unfortunately, there is simply no way to establish the existence of "oral traditions" at any particular moment in antiquity simply because, by their very nature, oral traditions leave no historical trace. As that is the case, the supposition that traditions existed orally prior to being written is open to neither verification nor negation, and therefore does nothing to further a secure conclusion about the antiquity of a given passage in the Torah.

Few scholars or religionists draw attention to the fact that the civilizations of the ancient Near East, dating back to the third millennium BCE, were all highly literate. The Sumerian and Akkadian civilizations preserved everything from trade agreements to poetry and literature in a sophisticated writing system known as cuneiform. Eventually, the alphabet was invented and proliferated among the Near Eastern cultures. In literate societies, important traditions get written down. This does not preclude origins in folk legends and myths that circulated within the cultural repertoire of the commoners; but the hypothesis that Israel's history and Mosaic legends could survive a millennium without being written—when in fact, a significant preoccupation of the Torah is *committing the covenant to writing*—seems unlikely.

One might ask, Doesn't dating the Torah to the fifth century BCE make it old enough? Being able to say that biblical literature comes (perhaps) from the time of Homer, written prior to Plato and Aristotle, strikes me as rather impressive. It still precedes the advent of Christianity by many centuries, and the appearance of Islam by more than a millennium. However, the notion of insisting upon a remote antiquity for the Torah's origins has a sociological explanation. The insistence on things like oral tradition developed hand-in-hand with the fading of Torah's original purpose and the emergence of a revamped usage: historiography. Once Jews (and eventually Christians) began to relate to their literature not *as literature*, but as a formal history, the quest for antiquity was intensified, largely because of misconceived notions that witnesses to history make the best historians.

First, though, let us turn to what Torah was *meant* to be before we consider the politics of both ancient and contemporary interpretations. I will offer here a very concise description of the Torah's history of composition.

Those interested in greater detail and depth can consult bibliographic works offered in the references.[1]

The Torah was written as a solution to a historical problem—the destruction of the Temple in 586 BCE and the emergence of a diasporic Jewish community whose identity could not be based exclusively, or even predominantly, upon the salience of the Land of Israel and its core institutions in Jewish life. Without a crisis in identity or religious ideas, there is no reason to create documents that focus on nurturing cultural distinctiveness. But a historical crisis of astounding magnitude is precisely what faced the authors of Torah. The Torah does not speak of a king; rather, it posits clan leaders as rulers at a local level, and a prophetic leader (Moses) as the highest authority. Moses, as a character, fits no paradigm of leadership known in any other Israelite or ancient Near Eastern literature.

We do, of course, find that an array of cultures had "prophets," but none ever promotes a prophet to the level of leadership enjoyed by Moses. As a literary construct, he constitutes a brilliant solution to what should have been an insurmountable problem: survival in an era after conquest without a king. The more usual historical pattern after a conquest ran like this: once a monarchy was removed and the central administration of an ancient society obliterated, a nation would be assimilated into the jurisdiction of the conqueror. Israel somehow managed to defy this paradigm of ancient life, and it did this, in part, by inventing its Torah. In this sense, the Torah represents among the most creative solutions to a historical problem ever proposed: the perpetuation of a civilization and the creation of a sense of social unity *through literature*.

Whether Abraham or Moses, Aaron or Joshua were the actual people the Torah stories are based upon, cannot be established. What can be said with certainty is that our stories about the biblical characters have very little to do with what modern students of history would call "history" and everything to do with the ideological agenda of the authors. Thus, even if these *were* all real historical figures, we are left with the literary representations of the Torah's authors, who readily fabricated personal conversations,

---

1. My own approach to the history of composition can be found in *Etched in Stone: The Emergence of the Decalogue* (New York: T. & T. Clark, 2006). See also E. Theodore Mullen Jr., *Ethnic Myths and Pentateuchal Foundations: A New Approach to the Formation of the Pentateuch* (Atlanta: Society of Biblical Literature, 1997); Mark Zvi Brettler, *The Creation of History in Ancient Israel* (London: Routledge, 1995); S. David Sperling, *The Original Torah: The Political Intent of the Bible's Writers* (New York: New York University Press, 1998).

reflections on motivations, and the discourse of intimate moments, none of which would have been invented by a "historian." The import of Torah lies in its ideological teachings and not in its historicity, of which it probably has very little.

For many people, this is disturbing. Disturbance over such a portrayal of Torah's origins derives from cultural prejudices and misconceptions about the relationship between fiction and truth. We regularly understand fictional literature as having the potential to capture and convey profound truths that no other medium manages to express. In fact, some of the most powerful confrontations with history itself take place through the medium of literary fiction. Elie Wiesel wrote *Night* and *Dawn* and *Gates of the Forest*, among other works, to tell the story of a Jew's experience during the Holocaust. Each of these volumes is written as a novel. If I really wanted someone to understand something about the Holocaust, I would never think to recommend first and foremost a history textbook; rather, I'd have someone start with Wiesel, or perhaps Thomas Keneally's novel *Schindler's Ark* (1982). Alternatively, I might consider recommending Steven Spielberg's film adaptation of this novel, *Schindler's List* (1993). Do you know of anyone who remarked, after seeing the film, that they considered it inadequate because it was nothing more than a reenactment based upon a novel? Do you know of anyone who discredited the importance of these works because dialogues and scenes were merely imaginative reconstructions of private or secluded moments that endeavored to capture the horrors of real-life history? Quite the contrary: we understand that novels (and films) are normally shaped according to the author's imagination and ideology. The story is able to transcend both time and place so as to capture truths about the human condition and history itself—truths that are exceedingly difficult to capture through other literary genres.

Now, I understand that some will object to this parallelism by proclaiming that these fictional adaptations nevertheless draw their meanings from real-life circumstances, in contrast to what I have suggested—and will be suggesting further in the essays that follow—that the episodes described in Torah never happened. Such a distinction could, indeed, prove fatal to my insistence that historical fiction can capture aspects of truth more powerfully than other genres of writing.

But in fact, this challenge proves irrelevant. Torah is an anthology of literary materials shaped to provide a future on the basis of a vision of the past. Torah is allegorical. It uses real-life circumstances—the circumstances of its target audience—as well as many fanciful events, to convey the culture's understanding of life and history's meaning. Its words are not meant to be read as literal representations of history; rather, we are to read its words for *the meanings its authors ascribe to the history they are living*. Relating to Torah as allegory was standard practice at various points in our history. It is only comparatively recently that we have lost our ability to read Torah for what it really is.

I remember reading an abridged version of Jonathan Swift's *Gulliver's Travels* as a child. It was wonderfully entertaining, but no child can possibly understand the sharp satirical approach to human nature and politics, or the parody of the travelogue genre, that motivated Swift—and I was surely no exception. It was only as an adult reading the original eighteenth-century version that I began to recognize Swift's cutting wit and critical insights. Of course, we instantly recognize that none of the phantasmagoric episodes in Swift's book actually happened. In one sense of the term "happened" this would be correct. But in another sense of the term, everything that Swift describes allegorically (and satirically) in his work was, indeed, taking place during his lifetime. The specific characters in the book may not have actually lived on earth, but they *represent* real people, or at least certain types of people at whom Swift aimed his critique. Allegory, then, is only meaningful if there is a reality to which it refers or corresponds. I will argue throughout these essays that Torah is not history, but that it is, in some very profound sense, an allegory for the reality experienced by the authors' audience. Too be yet more nuanced: Torah is about the reality the authors want their audience to experience. The earliest readers of Torah were supposed to associate their lives with the conditions met in the lives of their ancestors. When we read Torah, we do, in fact, read about real lives—those of the original authors' contemporaries.

Torah, of course, is not predominantly satirical or parodic—although it does contain passages of both—but like all complex texts, it can be read on multiple levels. The conviction sustained through these essays is that contemporary religious ideology should not trump the learning we gain through methods that involve credible means of verification and negation (sometimes called "the scientific method"). Liberal religious convictions, then, are to be formed on the basis of the best information available. When it comes to dating the origins of the Torah, there is no reason to assume that the core elements contained in the literature precede the redaction process by more than a couple of generations (if that). Should we, someday, find materials that help us achieve certainty regarding a more ancient period for the composition of any given story, we will be fortunate to have new parameters to embrace. But our critical learning also helps us understand that its qualities as a non-historical narrative—at least, non-historical in our modern sense of *history*—does not diminish its value as a religious or cultural object. History writing does not have a monopoly on meaning, nor is it the only way to describe reality.

Finally, a word about the "sanctity of the text." Over the years, I have heard people react to critical analyses of Torah with concern for how such an approach might undermine its sacredness. Equally troubling for some people is the notion that the text is altogether human in origins. Without some notion of a divine origin (whether it be godly dictation or that slippery word "inspiration"), some people believe there would be nothing more compelling about the Bible than any other great work of literature, whether it be Sophocles or Shakespeare.

Sacredness is a human product. Nothing is intrinsically holy. Sanctification requires an activity—that is, it is not a passive state of being. I do not believe it is at all a stretch to say that one's critical engagement with Torah can constitute an act of sanctification, if that notion should prove meaningful to a reader. What differentiates Shakespeare's works from Torah is not some intrinsic aspect related to origins or even the comparative qualities of the works. What differentiates various works of literature from one another is *the history of their reception* within a community. There are many great works of literature in the history of humankind, but only a handful has ever been engaged to spawn civilizations. What makes a given work compelling may have more to do with the unusual circumstances of its use in a given era than any particular qualities found on its pages. Indeed, many a great work has been lost to history, while many a mediocre verse has been preserved over millennia.

This is not the appropriate place for establishing the reasons one work was prolifically disseminated, another survived but remained obscure, and a third disappeared from history's stage within a generation of being penned. We study Torah because Torah has traversed millennia as a dynamic force in Western Civilization. It achieved canonical status within a discrete community, and it generated broad cultural trends. No two generations have ever read the Torah the same way, and from this it follows that we have no obligation to *receive* Torah the way any previous generation received it. For a literature to function dynamically and generatively at any given moment in history, it must be interpreted according to the most creative and critical tools available—creative with regard to unexplored meanings, and critical with regard to the needs of the generation at hand.

1

Thoughts on Method and Biblical Interpretation

UNDERSTANDING INTERPRETIVE STRATEGIES

Every time we pick up a text—whether it is a newspaper or a novel or the assembly directions for a bicycle—we engage an *interpretive strategy*. This is also true of every speech act we are part of, whether it be as passive listeners or active participants. Most of the time, that "strategy" functions in the background, just like the operating system and secondary programs on our computers. If we click on a "jpeg" file, we expect our computers to open up a program that will allow us to view or edit graphic images. That program, if you will, is our computer's strategy for viewing the file. If the computer's operating system were to try to open up our bank records with that same graphics editor, we'd immediately recognize that it had chosen the *wrong interpretive strategy* for that document.

We move seamlessly from using a word processor to an Internet web browser without paying any attention to the different "assumptions" those programs make about how they will best accomplish their tasks. In effect, the computer is structured so as to perceive certain clues in a file's format that will enable it to choose the best strategy for interpreting its "meanings." Our own brains work very much this way; or perhaps I should say that computer programming very much reflects the thinking process of its human creators and users. So, by way of analogy, we can say that an interpretive strategy is something like a computer program. And this analogy permits us to also say the following: just as no single computer program

9

will allow us to achieve all of our purposes, no single interpretive strategy will allow us to successfully interpret each and every text or utterance we come across in life.

The person who finds the comment "you will need a screw driver and wrench" among the assembly instructions for a bicycle is not expected to seek out deep, ironic meanings. That would clearly be a mistaken strategy. When talking with small children, our strategy for understanding their meanings and for speaking with them comprehensibly is quite different from the strategy we engage when talking with colleagues at work or with friends over dinner at a restaurant.

I started by saying that most of the time we engage a listening or reading strategy *in the background*. By that I meant we know automatically which strategy to use in well-rehearsed social or professional contexts. In a sense, these strategies are habitually engaged; as such, the "choice" is a matter of habit. When we are in unrehearsed or unfamiliar situations, we pick up signals as to which strategy will work best without having to make conscious decisions. These signals are often subtle and we perceive them on the basis of years of acculturated practice. The signals themselves are part of a broader system of characteristics that are often called "genre constraints." A genre is simply a *type* of literature (or art, or music, or even a kind of speech act) that consists of certain characteristics that are associated by convention. A formal lecture is a genre that entails certain characteristics that are quite different from those of a comic strip. Similarly, a text message sent from one's smartphone engages certain language features that would be both annoying and unsatisfactorily ambiguous if they were to be employed in the essay you are now reading. The characteristics that typify a genre function as constraints over what can be done or said within a given context. In a work of literature, one might think of those constraints as the encoded rules which the author and reader tacitly agree upon, so as to be able to communicate through writing.

LEARNING TO NAVIGATE EVER-SHIFTING GENRES

From childhood onward, we are acculturated into a world of genres and their constraints. When a child hears the words "Once upon a time," she immediately knows a certain kind of story is about to unfold. She also learns to relate to that story in a certain "make-believe" way. Some of these understandings are taught to her, and others she learns over time on the basis of her own powers of induction and deduction, and also by emulating the interpretive acts of older children and adults. With time, we expect her to choose the right strategy for responding to the phrase "Once upon a time" (*It's make-believe!*) and we expect her to understand that the strategy she uses for that phrase will not be appropriate for the phrase "It's bedtime now!" (where the comment is usually meant literally).

There is little purpose in trying to rigidly define those characteristics that form a genre or that contribute to its detection. We can speak of a murder mystery, a romance, a university lecture, a creation story in the Bible, or a thank-you note as all being formed on the basis of genre constraints, but none of these genres (or any other, for that matter) entails a finite set of fixed characteristics or rules. Rather, we discern genres on the basis of typical characteristics or conditions that, over time, we come to learn (and expect) through experience or direct instruction. In effect, we discern genres on the basis of a preponderance of characteristics. Like culture in general, genres are constantly shifting, or to express that more technically: over time, a genre's typical characteristics change. Some of those changes will be stylistic, others will be more substantive, as when they are related to plot or to character and gender depictions.

Most of the time, genre shifts (like cultural change) are slow and gradual, or involve small aspects of a genre, and this is what allows us to feel comfortable reading works that were written before our own lifetimes. For instance, detective novels from the early nineteenth century had exclusively male protagonists. Then there appeared "Mrs. Gladden," the first-person narrator of *The Female Detective* (1864) and a new genre was born.[1] However, this genre did not undergo its most serious transformation until the 1970s, in books by (mostly) women novelists. That is to say, at an early moment in the genre's history, female detectives first appeared, and yet it took quite a while for the genre to reach its most developed stage, during the "second wave" of feminism.[2] Although Mrs. Gladden first appeared in 1864, most of the other typical characteristics of this genre remained stable for quite some time.

Someone reading today might not be aware of how unusual the appearance of a female detective would have seemed to certain generations

---

1. See Kathleen Klein, *The Woman Detective: Gender & Genre*, 2nd ed. (Champaign: University of Illinois Press, 1995).

2. See Priscilla L. Walton and Manina Jones, *Detective Agency: Women Rewriting the Hard-Boiled Tradition* (Berkeley: University of California Press, 1999).

of readers. That's because we only rarely read with a sense of a genre's history intact. Rather, we learn to adapt to the shifting characteristics of genre unconsciously, just as we interpret new idioms that a friend or colleague might use casually in conversation. Over time, we accept shifts in genre constraints as readily as we accept new idioms in colloquial speech. After a very short time, those new idioms are no longer "new," and the same is true of ever-changing genre constraints. The innovative approach of one author may become a standard practice within a brief generation of writers and readers.

THINKING ABOUT ACCOMMODATING
MORE SIGNIFICANT GENRE SHIFTS

Now let's complicate things a bit more. Let's consider, say, a novel written in 2016 that we would readily recognize as a romance. Surely it will share a great many characteristics with a romance written just five years earlier. What happens when we compare that 2008 work with a book written in 1850? In order for us to relate to them both as romances, they must have enough characteristics in common to be recognizable as such. We might decide, for instance, that a romance must involve a sense of destiny; that lovers must encounter obstacles to the fulfillment of that destiny. We might decide that the main characters have a certain appearance or that antagonists behave and look a certain way. Just how much two works must have in common so as to fit our genre expectations at any given moment is a subjective matter. One person may feel that a romance that ends unhappily violates the most important element of this particular genre (pushing it toward "tragedy"), while another person may feel that a happy ending is not a necessary condition for a work to constitute a romance. And then there are works of literature we might view as "genre-hybrids," where the characteristics of two (or perhaps even more) genres coalesce in a single, extended narrative.

While this may be a subjective judgment, it obviously has implications as to which interpretive strategy people will consider engaging for their respective reading experiences. If two people have radically different strategies for reading a single work, then their understandings of that work will differ significantly. You can begin to see why this might prove important to our own engagement with biblical literature. If you and I begin this series of essays on Genesis believing radically different things about the genre constraints at work in this literature, then we are not likely to communicate very well regarding the potential meanings of this biblical book. Yet decisions regarding genre are going to be required at every turn of the reading experience. Consider the conflicting interpretations that would result if one interpreter viewed a given passage as allegorical and another viewed it as a literal history. For instance, is the story of Joseph as second-in-command in Egypt to be taken as a historically accurate portrayal of actual events, or was this story composed according to the constraints of what we might now call a "fantasy" genre? Is Jacob's wrestling match at Jabbok literally a confrontation with a divine being, or is the entire episode symbolic? Obviously, the tools engaged to interpret an allegory are quite distinct from those that work well for understanding historiography. There needs to be some basis for establishing our interpretive strategy so that our interpretations might prove meaningful *and* plausible.

At one level, much of literary criticism entails debating which reading strategy will best suit a given work. Resolving this debate with regard to biblical literature is not our task in this context. However, I want it to be clear from the onset what assumptions are at work in my comments, primarily so that they will make sense to you, the reader, but also so that they might prove *useable* by you as you read other biblical passages. While I believe my reading strategy offers a rich yield, I am not offering a critique of other strategies, some of which might prove equally valuable. That critique would require a survey of scholarly engagements with the history of interpretation rather than an interpretation of Torah itself.

ANTIQUITY, TRANSLATIONS, AND THE HISTORICAL-CRITICAL METHOD

I noted above that sometimes we need to consciously learn some things about a genre or a literary work specifically in order to make sense of it. This is especially true when we are dealing with documents that derive from cultures or eras other than our own. For instance, few of us are able to pick up and read successfully a play by Shakespeare without having acquired some additional training. Both the language and the forms of the dramas themselves are outside of the common contemporary cultural repertoire. The amount of formal training required to master a new genre has a great deal to do with how different it is from those genres already in our personal repertoires. A narrative deriving from the distant past is not likely to have very much in common with contemporary literary forms. This can even be the case when our culture is, genealogically speaking, a remote descendant of the cultural context that gave birth to a text we consider our own. Moreover, anything from the distant past was written in a language quite different from our vernacular, and this serves to increase the degree of unfamiliarity.

When children meet a new genre for the first time, they quite automatically engage whatever interpretive tools are at their disposal and plunge ahead. For the most part, they are not bothered by the types of indeterminacies that disturb us as adults. In fact, they may not even identify those elements that are at odds with their understanding level as everything gets folded into their imaginative worldview. This is the magic of childhood. Over time, we want children to master ever more sophisticated interpretive strategies in order to understand more about our world. In order to do that, they must constantly accrue new interpretive strategies. We teach them, for instance, that there is a difference between a "make believe" story and a story that tells us the history of something. They come to expect that Harry Potter doesn't really attend Hogwarts, but that the writer of these comments does actually teach at a real-life school in the United States. They come to understand that imaginative play is different from playing a game, where set rules must be mastered.

As adult readers confronted with a new genre, our first reaction is to engage whatever interpretive tools are in our toolbox of strategies, not unlike children. We are acculturated to force even the unfamiliar into familiar rubrics. In some contexts, we adapt what's available and end up navigating new scenarios just fine because the amount of dissimilarity is easily accommodated. In other contexts, however, we sense that the tools we have at our disposal are inadequate for a particular interpretive task. We may become frustrated by our inability to make sense of what we are reading or seeing.

In some contexts, we are fooled into believing that our tools are adequate for a given interpretive process even when they are, in fact, quite inadequate. I dare say, this is as true of the scholar as it is the common reader. A false sense of confidence is particularly common when we read ancient literatures in translation. By their very nature, translations are designed to *transfer the sense* of a text, as the translator interprets its meanings. Once we hold a book in translation in our hands we quickly come to feel as if we are reading a narrative that emerged from our own language and culture. That, of course, is the translator's goal. But this sense of security can induce an interpretive confidence that will result in an impoverished reading experience. Is this a bad thing? Well, it depends upon your goals. If you believe that a translator can adequately capture the meanings of a text in a foreign language, then you might not think twice about engaging a translation. However, those who know more than one language readily appreciate just how difficult it can be to translate certain expressions or to capture poetic imagery both concisely and truthfully. Moreover, if you are seeking life-meanings, or guidelines for setting up a community, or simply a perspective on your people's history as reflected in an ancient book, then achieving *as rich a reading* as possible is probably a high priority. Such readings will require coming to terms with the problems of deciphering an ancient language, ancient literary genres, and the ancient cultural repertoires behind those genres.

I do not want to get into a long excursus on the theory of translation in this context. Nor would I be ready to quantify, in the case of any given Hebrew passage I myself have translated, just how much of the text's meanings and resonances were captured successfully, and how much was left behind. But I do want it to be clear that the literature we will be reading together—biblical literature—derives from a distant world and was penned in a language that is not our vernacular (and this would be no less true for an Israeli whose mother tongue is modern rather than biblical Hebrew).

I readily admit that I am a believer in the *possibility* of translation. I have no doubt whatsoever that among contemporary languages, we can capture a large portion of the meanings intended by an author or speaker who works in a language different from our own. That said, I also readily acknowledge that literature in any language invariably conveys imagery and subtle meanings that are specific to the resonances of a particular language and culture, making them altogether untranslatable. Add to this conundrum the fact that ancient languages invariably complicate matters even further, due to our inability to reconstruct certain idioms or images, and one begins to frame the nature of a translation's limitations. Let me provide one example. In biblical narrative, if someone is walking along and happens to see something, the phrase we expect to find in Hebrew is *vayisa' 'et 'eynav.* In the King James English translation of 1611, this was rendered literally as "he lifted up his eyes." Because of the cultural prowess of that translation, we've actually become acclimated to hearing this phrase, even though its literal meaning is nonsense. Were it not for its idiomatic acceptance the phrase should simply have been translated as "he looked up" or even "he came upon" or "he promptly noticed." Idiomatic phrases do not use words according to their literal meanings. When we say, "Pay attention!" we do not hear the word "pay" as having anything to do with a monetary transaction. In modern Hebrew, to say "pay attention" you literally say, "place [your] heart"; there is no word parallel to "pay" present in the idiom. Were someone to translate the modern Hebrew *sim lev* into English as "place [your] heart" rather than "pay attention," we would recognize it as a mis-translation. In that sense, the literal rendering "he lifted up his eyes" is equally mistaken.

Of course, we cannot be certain whether the native ancient Hebrew speaker heard something in particular in any given idiom, and this is part of the problem we face in trying to reconstruct meanings in ancient languages. Confounding this issue of semantics even further is the layer of meaning or resonance acquired through literary artistry. There is a difference between translating a common conversation, or even simple prose, and rendering works of what we might call "high literature," where language is used in a particularly self-conscious, even lofty manner, whether in poetry or prose. In literature we expect a writer to employ highly stylized expressions and various literary techniques (such as foreshadowing or allegory); we expect an author to pay attention to syntactic variation, assonance (how phrases sound), and aesthetic elements that generally do not find their way into bicycle-assembly instruction manuals. Just how much of a text's "meaning" is conveyed by the sounds of the words chosen by the author, by a particular idiom, or in the relationship between various words in languages that use strong root systems is extremely difficult (if not impossible) to quantify. Moreover, while some of the elements that inspire us to classify a work of writing as "literature" can be adequately executed in translations (especially the more structural elements, such as allegory or foreshadowing), those that are more language-based—such as idiomatic expressions, assonance, word-play, and even metaphors that are culture-specific—are virtually impossible to render in a foreign tongue. Because we sense that language in literature is more self-consciously formulated than in other kinds of usage, we can readily understand why a more schooled interpretive strategy may be required to produce a meaningful reading of any document recognized as literary.

Even when we think we can understand every word in a sentence, the worldview of the Bible's target audience was so different from our own that interpretive confidence is hard to muster. One of the scholar's primary tasks is to research the cultural perspectives that were part of the original author's world. Generally we believe that the more we can understand about the author's world, the greater our chances are of offering sound interpretations of her or his work. But then, "even the simplest statement," suggests George Steiner, "does not pass unaltered into another language; each language frames the world uniquely."[3]

My goal here is not to discourage anyone from reading a book in translation or to undermine our ability to excavate the meanings of ancient texts. We can only be expected to give it our best effort on the basis of the most informed platform we can acquire. But that is exactly the point. I started these comments by noting that we all engage an interpretive strategy at every single moment that we are called upon to interpret something. I have now introduced complicating factors, such as a text originally written in a foreign language or in the distant past. Both of these factors imply that the cultural repertoire at the author's disposal was quite different from our own. These are precisely the contexts in which we may assume that our standard tools of interpretation will yield compromised results, therefore leading us to conclude that additional training may be required to make the reading experience more satisfying. But even then, translations and interpretations are not equivalences of an original work. Again, to quote George Steiner, a translation is "a vital counterpoise, an echo, faithful yet autonomous, as we find in the dialogue of human love. An act of translation is an act of love. Where it fails, through immodesty or blurred perception, it traduces. Where it succeeds, it incarnates" (271).

These sentiments are not without controversy when expressed regarding the Hebrew Bible. There are many people who believe that the Bible was written in such a way as to embrace eternal truths and messages that are unchanging and readily accessible throughout the ages. The Torah and other biblical books were translated into Greek early in the third century BCE, within 250 years of its completion, and into Aramaic (in multiple versions) not long thereafter. Additional Greek renderings appeared during the Roman era, and eventually Latin translations as well. By the eighth century of the Common Era, the Bible had multiple translations in Aramaic and even Arabic. This was not the case in Christian Europe. The Catholic Church, which advocated exclusively on behalf of its official Latin rendition, refused to allow the Bible to be translated into the vernacular

3. George Steiner, *Language and Silence: Essays on Language, Literature, and the Inhuman*, Atheneum 158 (New Haven: Yale University Press, 1970) 270.

languages of Europe so that it could enjoy a monopoly on its exposition. Common Christians, unlearned in Latin, had no direct access to the biblical text except through Church-designated mediators of the text (priests) until the very first translations appeared. The fourteenth century saw the emergence of Bible translations into an array of languages (for example, in English, John Wyclif, 1383/1400; in German, the Wenzel Bible of 1389); however, they drew from the Latin rendering known as the Vulgate rather than from the original Hebrew. The same was true of the widely influential translations by William Tyndale into English in 1525, by Jacques Lefèvre d'Étaples into French in 1530, and Martin Luther into German in 1534. The primary intent of all these translators was the proliferation of Bible readings among common folk. Tyndale and Luther, not to mention those who worked before them, lived under considerable peril, as their work was opposed by the Catholic Church.

It was not long before people related to their translations as the authentic text of the Bible itself. And since people feel quite comfortable with their vernacular, there appeared to be no interpretive barriers between the average literate person and the meanings of biblical literature. It is still frequently the case that people who are habitual readers of the Bible do not recognize that the original version of the Torah was written in Hebrew, or that the original version of Christian Scriptures (the New Testament) appeared first in Greek. And without that recognition, there is no reason to sense that the literature is either "foreign" or culturally at odds with our own times.

Jews have long related to the Hebrew text of the Tanakh (an acronym standing for the three divisions of the Hebrew Bible: Torah, Prophets, Writings) through translations and commentaries. So the fact that we will study Torah together through a translation—in this case, English—has historical precedents dating back to the Hellenistic Era. Indeed, the first systematic exposition of Torah written by a Jew was composed in Greek by Philo Judaeus (20 BCE–50 CE), who knew no Hebrew.

My reason for highlighting the problems with reading a text from the ancient world and in translation was to put in place the very particular strategy for interpreting Torah that will be evident throughout these essays. I want it to be clear from the start that, despite the comfort we may feel when the Torah is in our hands in a familiar English rendering, the text is of an ancient and foreign origin. Part of my intention is to emphasize the strangeness of the text, so as to break stereotypical readings and to push us toward more insightful considerations of the underlying messages of various passages.

For those who believe that the Torah is the word of God, the only "intent" that is important to them is God's own. If God is the author, then the messages of Torah must not only be eternal but accessible, for God must have wanted there to be translations. It should be clear by now that this is not an attitude that will inform the comments I will offer on the various themes of the book of Genesis. Humans write texts, not gods. There is nothing divine about the Torah except insofar as divinity is central to the mythology of the story. Rather, the Torah is a highly charged political, ethnic, and religious document, and part of our goal will be to explore how the ancients understood the role of literature in developing ethnic identity, shoring up political power, and establishing religious practice. I consider these aspects to be the most exhilarating features of the Torah, for it is by elucidating the various purposes of Torah that we are forced to think though our own engagement with the issues of today, and perhaps more important, how literature might serve the same vibrant function in our age as it did in antiquity.

CRITICISM AND IDEOLOGY

Authorial intent is what we are after when we first approach a text. However, there is no question that a text can have meanings that an author did not intend. This is to acknowledge that the overwhelming majority of engagements with language (spoken and written) are imperfect and entail innumerable indeterminacies. Many ambiguities are irresolvable; others can be worked through, although perhaps never fully. Despite acknowledging these indeterminacies, I still find the endeavor of engaging a text from antiquity worthwhile, even as I surrender any hope of establishing an interpretive strategy that might yield a "perfect reading." Indeed, there is no such thing as a perfect reading. There are bad readings and there are good readings. Some good readings are better than others, and some bad readings are worse than others. We can measure the merits of readings against one another, but we have no way to retrieve our ancient authors to verify just how close our readings are to their intentions.

What, then, will our shared strategies be in this context? The first step in the consideration of each passage will be to establish the core of an informed reading. By "an informed reading" I mean an interpretation of a passage that emerges on the basis of a variety of language- and literature-related scholarly tools of potential relevance. Once that is in place, we can begin to build a sustained discussion of what the Torah authors were endeavoring to create through their literature. In contemporary settings, we may not think of literature as trying to *create something* outside of its own narrative world. But biblical literature is quite intently focused on having an impact upon the organization and character of the society for which it is written. Indeed, the impact it seeks to have on the society of its own day and subsequent generations is comparable to the impact the authors of the American Constitution sought to have over American society in perpetuity. Each of the books of the Hebrew Bible, like the Constitution, is an ideological work, and consequently, understanding its inner working requires reading strategies that may not be relevant to most other instances of literary interpretation. To that end, I wish to introduce the idea of *criticism* more formally, and the notion of *ideological criticism* in particular.

Whenever the word "criticism" is used with regard to classical literatures, it connotes an analytical approach that fuses theory about literature with theory about culture, society, and politics more generally. That is, we take the word to connote a *formal analytical* kind of discourse rather than some more generic "evaluation" of a work's success. In common parlance, most people associate the word "critique" with a book or film review, and it is this idea that I wish to distance from the more scholarly use of the term *criticism*. A "critique" in *The New York Times Book Review* section (ostensibly) evaluates how successfully a book is written: Is it interesting? Is the plot well formed? Is the use of language particularly artistic or skilled? Similarly, movie reviews are often written to help us decide whether we will like or dislike viewing a particular film. Literary criticism of the kind we will employ here—and by extension, cultural criticism—does not deal with likes and dislikes (except, perhaps, as a historical observation). Rather, literary criticism scrutinizes the ideas and forms of literary works, as well as their impact on everything from the politics to the social customs of a given era.

Some cultural and literary critics view the function of criticism as a struggle against the unspoken and unquestioned beliefs that permeate a society. The critic exposes these beliefs and sheds light on how they function as control mechanisms serving the interests of those who have power in a given society. When understood this way, criticism is not simply a scholarly endeavor, it is also a political engagement.[4] Frequently, a cluster

---

4. For an exposition of this theme, see Terry Eagleton's *The Function of Criticism*, (London: Verso, 1984).

of beliefs functions for an individual or within a society as an *ideology*. My goal here is not to provide a history of this extremely complex notion. For our purposes, I shall define ideology in such a way as to make it most useful for our own consideration of themes in the book of Genesis.

Louis Althusser suggested that ideology is about ideas and beliefs *manifest in practice*. We believe certain things that we simply pick up throughout life without ever challenging them, and those things we believe shape our conduct in an array of social, political, and religious contexts. The intelligentsia may reflect upon the core sources and meanings of culture, but the common person simply *behaves* in certain ways on the basis of an unreflective (and largely passive) process of acculturation.[5] As Terry Eagleton explains it, "The great majority of people believe without knowing that they do." Belief without knowledge is this very notion of living within a culture without consciously reflecting upon the constraints, customs, and structures that comprise it. We refer to that amalgam of beliefs which shape people's actions as *an ideology*.

Admittedly, there is an unavoidable circularity to understanding ideology in this manner. On the one hand, our beliefs and actions form a unity we call culture. That is, our beliefs define what we view as morally right, what we see as beautiful, what we hold as obligations and rights, what we classify as holy and profane. As such it might sound as if our beliefs *are* our culture, and our culture is *made up of* our beliefs. But, in fact, it is more complicated than that. Our quietly held beliefs are not all acquired arbitrarily or randomly. Many are intentionally promulgated by various forces in a society. Today we study the impact of various media—such as television, the Internet, publications, film—as key influences upon and shapers of a culture. We trace the genealogy of an idea to its source so as to expose who influences its proliferation. Moreover, we are interested in understanding how the content and form of the media affect what people believe.

It is quite common to view media today as competing brokers in an alleged marketplace of ideas. Which ones, if any, will come to dominate is difficult to predict. In past generations, the number of brokers in the idea game were fewer. This was especially the case in antiquity, when literacy was limited and the avenues for dissemination of information were not only drastically less than what is available today, but largely controlled by a very concentrated cluster of powerful individuals. Of course, we all know

---

5. Louis Althusser, *Lenin and Philosophy* (1971) 167, as discussed in Terry Eagleton, *The Idea of Culture*, Blackwell Manifestos (Malden, MA: Blackwell, 2000) 114–15.

of societies today where every form of media and self-expression is strictly controlled by government oversight, drastically diminishing the availability of ideas beyond those sanctioned by the ruling powers. But aside from these extreme contexts, our own world is far more complicated when it comes to the availability of information than anything known to the premodern era. Thus, the circularity I refer to is actually less round than it might otherwise appear. There are sources behind the ideas that are transmitted in every literary work in antiquity, and those sources are invariably working on behalf of some patron's interests. All writing emerged on the basis of patronage, and no patron commissioned a scribe without a social, religious, or political agenda in place. As such, the ideas that make up an era's dominant ideology are also neither arbitrary nor random; indeed, they are quite planned.

Ideological criticism, then, endeavors to uncover that set of unspoken beliefs that shaped how a literature was written and read early in its history of circulation. Often, underlying ideas are implied rather than spelled out directly, while in other contexts, an author makes quite clear how he or she intends to shape an audience's beliefs and attitudes. The book of Genesis entails one dominant school of thought regarding the origins and purpose of ancient Israel. The understanding of Genesis that will be pursued in these pages is quite specifically focused on the ideology that both shaped and was promoted by the book's author (or authors, as the case may be). If we wield our tools successfully, they should expose for us a Genesis Ideology at work in each segment of the book's narrative agenda.

2

Immortality Missed

Genesis 1–3

We regularly distinguish common stories from those we consider *mythic*. The philosopher Paul Ricoeur suggested that this distinction is useful for recognizing that myth manages to express profound ideas about what we perceive to be fundamental aspects of reality. At the same time, mythic thinking includes recognition of the fact that we cannot know reality in any complete sense. Thus, we convey what we *believe* to be true through symbols and imageries, the building blocks of literature and the arts. In effect, myth enables us say what we feel we know, even when that knowledge remains less than certain.

The opening stories of Genesis are most certainly mythic in this sense. However, they have undergone a number of editorial transformations that obscure aspects of their original intent. I do not believe these revisions were devised to *de*mythologize the original stories, as some scholars maintain. Rather, the editors here, as elsewhere in Genesis, merged various aspects of their literary inheritance with the intent of leaving us a narrative that was at its core an anthology. This practice was not uncommon among ancient Near Eastern cultures.

I want to elucidate two aspects of Genesis 1–3 that have been partially obscured by that anthologizing process. First, within Israelite literature there were competing ideological camps regarding the depiction of God. One ideology we would recognize as strictly monotheistic, where monotheism is the belief that there is only one God; the other should be defined as *monolatristic*. Monolatry is the belief that a supreme deity, often referred to by the Hebrew letters *YHWH* (which I will render *Yahweh*), is

23

responsible for Israel, but other gods, which are aligned with other peoples, also exist.[1] Israel did not develop from monolatry to monotheism along a straight path. Rather, these two notions of God probably existed side-by-side for quite some time. Our Bible preserves passages typical of both schools of thought. Monotheism eventually became a core and dominant belief within Judaism, and the literary vestiges of other beliefs were simply read through monotheistic lenses.

The second idea I wish to explore is only understandable against the backdrop of monolatry, and that is the issue addressed by the Adam and Eve story: our mortality. As we shall see, when scrutinized on the basis of its clear monolatristic imagery, the story proves to be a profound elucidation of humankind's failure to achieve immortality—what the author believed was very much within our potential, if but for a brief moment in time.

Our understanding of this first chapter will be quite different if we reconceptualize its expressions in harmony with ancient Near Eastern literatures. The notion that God created simply by speaking is central to the epic known as *Enuma Elish*, a Mesopotamian story of divine intrigue, combat, and creation. In *Enuma Elish*, the god Marduk is proclaimed the supreme deity by a cluster of deities engaged in a revolt against the divine establishment. Demonstrating his powers before his subordinates, Marduk speaks and brings various things into existence, just as Yahweh, Israel's God, speaks in Genesis 1 and brings the world into existence. In effect, our biblical author has Yahweh emulating—and at some level, replacing—Marduk as creator, by using his same technique. Moreover, *Enuma Elish* and other Mesopotamian legends make clear that the gods created human beings to serve them, and that those humans (as we shall see) physically resembled gods. Finally, gods in Mesopotamian legends become weary when they are engaged in strenuous endeavors (especially warfare). The plot of Enuma Elish tells the story of elder deities complaining about the noise made by adolescent gods, making it impossible to rest at night. The Israelite god, Yahweh, also seeks rest, as we are told in Exodus 31:17: "For Yahweh created the heavens and the earth in six days; on the seventh he ceased and revived himself." The power of God in Genesis 1, then, may

---

1. The word *Yahweh* is a transliteration of the name of God known as the tetragrammaton, or "four letter" name. In most scholarly tracts, the "w" stands for the letter today spoken as "vav," that is, a "v" rather than a "w" sound. However, it is speculated that the original sound of this letter was, indeed, closer to a "w," as it is pronounced in Arabic, whereas the "v" sound was associated with the letter *bet* (ב, when it lacked a *dagesh*) only. I will conform to the common spelling practice among scholars in these essays.

have partially been communicated to the ancient reader when he is depicted as fashioning the world non-stop over six consecutive days without respite. The modern reader, for whom God is omnipotent and requires no sleep, would have no notion that any deity required rest. With that ideology in place, such a reader would never imagine that the author of Genesis 1 was depicting his deity as a Super-God by emphasizing his extraordinary powers of endurance: six days of incessant creation. But this was part of the project of differentiating the Israelite God from the other deities—Yahweh, as guardian of Israel, would not slumber (Psalm 121:3).

Now, I am *not* saying that Genesis 1 reads precisely or even predominantly the way other ancient Near Eastern creation stories read. There are many differences, and they are important to highlight. However, certain basic themes apparent in Genesis are clearly drawn from a cultural repertoire that was shared throughout the ancient Near East. For instance, that Israel's God, Yahweh, was not alone when the world was created emerges explicitly in a few verses, especially 1:26 and 3:22. The former reads: "Elohim (i.e., God or perhaps *the gods*) said, 'Let us make a being who will have our form and our appearance.'" The form of the verb, *na'aseh*, expresses a first-person plural subject. The first person plural also appears in verse 3:22, which reads: "Yahweh of the gods said, 'The human has become just like us, cognizant of good and evil. Should he reach and eat of the Tree of Eternal Life, he will become immortal.'"

One of the words for "God" in Hebrew is, oddly enough, a plural word, *'elohim*. Unfortunately, we cannot explain how this plural noun came to mean "God" in the singular. But the expression "*YHWH* Elohim" is likely a reflection of an earlier ideology that understood *Yahweh* to be the principal deity amidst a pantheon of lesser gods. This is the idea we hear in the biblical phrase taken from Exodus 15:11, "Who is like you, Yahweh, *among the gods?*" The answer to this rhetorical question is not "there are no other gods," but rather, "no god is like you, Yahweh." Biblical verses reflecting this particular worldview are numerous.

When monotheism finally came on the scene, it did so with a vengeance. There are many passages whose primary goal is to counter non-monotheistic ideologies. For instance, in 2 Samuel 7:22 we read: "You are great, Lord Yahweh, for there are none like you, nor are there gods other than you!" Notice how this author engaged the notion of "like you" as we find it in Exodus 15, but then elucidated its meaning by demanding that there are no other gods. Similarly, the writer of Isaiah 45, who was a vehement advocate of monotheism, wrote unequivocally in God's voice: "I am Yahweh, and there are no other gods besides me!" No one expends energy arguing against ideas that have no adherents. Based on the vehemence of the monotheistic argument in the writings of certain authors, we can assume that monotheism was not Israel's original ideology. Moreover, it may not have been its dominant belief system for quite some time, even though it would eventually become a signature element of the Jewish religion.

Accepting that certain aspects of our first three chapters of Genesis were written by someone comfortable with a monolatristic belief system, we now turn to the role of those verses cited above: Genesis 1:26 and 3:22. What is the purpose of the Adam and Eve story? Various later editors grafted onto the original narrative core a variety of themes that were foreign to the earliest mythological material. If we clear away those various additions, we end up with a legend that instructs us as to the difference between humans and gods.

In ancient Near Eastern religions, gods were immortal but not necessarily eternal. By that I mean: gods *could* live forever, but they could also be killed. The epic mentioned above, *Enuma Elish*, describes combat among the immortal gods, which results in the death of two particularly significant deities, Tiamat and Qingu. Tiamat is the Mother Goddess of creation—of the world of gods, that is. Her offspring would eventually create humans as servants (as recorded in a variety of other ancient stories). This helps us understand the intent of that verse in Genesis 1:26, which depicts the deities coming together to make a being that was fundamentally like themselves—offspring, if you will. Humans, then, look just like gods, but they differ, both in the knowledge that they have or could have, and in their lack of immortality.

The serpent in our story correctly perceives that the gods have subjected the first humans to a ruse. The threats of instantaneous death upon consuming from the Tree of Knowledge are quite untrue. Had Adam and Eve eaten of both trees in the center of the garden, they would have been transformed into the equivalent of deities. But since they only ate of the Tree of Knowledge, they were left with but *two-thirds* of a god's characteristics. That is, they were created to look like gods (having been created in their image), and they acquired the ethical discernment of gods as a result of having eaten of the Tree of Knowledge. However, having failed to grab the fruit of eternal life before being banished from Eden, they did not acquire immortality.

Many of these details are shared with stories in other ancient cultures. For instance, Gilgamesh, King of Uruk (ancient Babylon), is also two-thirds god and one-third human.[2] Just as in the Genesis story, the missing third is permanence itself. After witnessing the murder of his closest friend, Enkidu, by the jealous goddess Ishtar, Gilgamesh sets out to find the secret of eternal life so as to avoid Enkidu's fate. The only way to fend off the possibility of death is through the consumption of a certain "plant of rejuvenation," which allows one to regain youth so as to live again with the wisdom acquired over the years. Gilgamesh, unsure as to the effects of eating the plant, hesitates to consume it. At that moment of hesitation, a snake sneaks up and carries the plant off. In effect, his delayed action proves to be his undoing.

The similarity of narrative elements between the Gilgamesh and biblical narratives are blatant enough. Just as Gilgamesh achieves two-thirds of divine likeness, Adam and Eve are also, in effect, two-thirds gods. But, because they fail to eat of the plant of immortality, they, like Gilgamesh, fail to acquire that final third. Both stories involve a serpent, although the serpent's deeper cultural significance remains ambiguous.

Despite their similarities, these stories represent two very different ways of narrating this core mythic theme. If we peel away the various strata placed upon the chapters by later authors, I think we can come close to reconstructing the original core story as follows:

> The gods said, "Let us make humans [to serve us] that resemble us in appearance and form [only lacking understanding and immortality]." The gods did just that: they created the creature known as *adam* to resemble themselves in appearance—male and female . . .
>
> Yahweh, the chief god, placed the male and female in the Garden of Eden and said, "Of every tree in the garden you are free to eat; but as for the Tree of Knowledge of Good and Evil, you shall not consume its fruit. *As soon as you eat of it, you shall die.*"
>
> Now the serpent, being shrewd [grasped the divine ruse]. He approached the woman and said, "Did God say, 'You shall not eat of the trees of the garden?'" The woman replied to the serpent, "We may eat of the fruit of the garden trees, only regarding the tree in the middle of the garden, God said, 'You shall neither eat of it nor touch it, lest you die.'"
>
> The serpent responded, "[This is not true. If you eat of that tree] you are not going to die. [The gods know that as soon as you

2. See Tablet I, line 46.

27

eat of that tree you will grasp what is good and evil and you will become just like gods.]"

The woman ate of the Tree of Knowledge and did not die. She shared the fruit of that tree with the man, and he did not die. At that moment, Yahweh, supreme among the gods, was moving about the garden. The man and woman hid. Yahweh called to them. Upon finding them, he suspected that they had eaten of the Tree of Knowledge.

To the other gods Yahweh proclaimed, "Now that man and woman have become like us in knowing good and evil, should he stretch out his hand and take from the Tree of Immortality, he will [rival us] and live forever!" At that moment, Yahweh drove them out of the garden and prevented their return by stationing cherubim and a fiery, ever-turning sword to guard access to the Tree of Immortality.

(verses drawn from Genesis 1:26–31, 2:15—3:24)

I offer this as a reconstruction of the core story, upon which were grafted the ideas of nakedness as inappropriate, sin, and deception, along with the resulting punishments that now define the human condition (pain in childbirth, relentless working of the land, etc.). But the core story strikes me as more focused and more profound than the final redacted version. It forces us to reflect upon just how much of life is as it is because of opportunities missed, because of hesitancy at moments that required boldness, because of our failures to scrutinize the truth of what we are told. And who among us, confronted with our own finitude, will not find this yearning for immortality-missed, poignant even today?

3

Family Trees, Branches, and Identity

Genesis 19

The book of Genesis involves a patchwork of stories. These are held together by an overarching framework that I shall refer to as "the ideological overlay." How are we to understand this structure? Picture eggs in an egg crate. When open, the box is flimsy and the eggs all sit there as discrete and unconnected entities. When closed, such that the eggs are touching the top and bottom surfaces of those spaces specially designed to hold them, the structure becomes rigid and you relate to the sum of the parts—the crate and the eggs—as a solid whole. In this analogy, the eggs are the discrete stories that make up the book of Genesis and the crate constitutes the structural framework that holds the individual stories together. Just as an egg crate, when closed, feels pretty solid, so does the book of Genesis looked at as a whole—its narratives flow "solidly" from one part to the next. The narrative appears to have been written as if all of its parts belonged together, from beginning to end. However, when we peel back the ideological overlay—opening the egg crate—we become conscious that the distinct stories share neither a thematic unity nor a chronological integrity. Just as your egg crate contains eggs that didn't start out together, so it is that the stories in Genesis did not start out clustered together as they currently are. Rather, the sense of unity was created by the book's editor.

The stories the editor decided to include address a great array of concerns, but two main thematic elements lend the entire work narrative and ideological unity. The first element consists of those periodic genealogies we read; the second is what we might call "the Covenant Ideology." We will meet this second element in our next chapter. In the present context, we will focus on the very important genealogy that traces the regeneration of humanity after the devastating flood of Noah's era. The repopulation of the world leads to the ancestry we identify with ancient Israel.[1]

The Genesis genealogies define both the lineage of the world's nations and Israel's place in that world. Identity in antiquity was frequently developed around two notions: blood relations and land. When it came to familial or tribal units, establishing what was meant by "We" frequently involved defining some "Other" group. In effect, people declared what or who they were by articulating what or who they were not. *We* form a group; *they* are not part of our group.

This approach to self-differentiation is not without certain inner paradoxes. The Bible seeks to show that all human beings derive first from Adam and Eve, and then from Noah's sons and daughters-in-law. In other words, we are all, in some sense, *related,* and consequently, differentiation among peoples proves to be a tricky business. The paradox, then, lies in the notion that the writers were moved to valorize some groups and villainize others, despite the fact that heroes and villains may only have had a few degrees of blood-line separation between them.

Then there is the problem of ever-shifting attitudes toward discrete ethnic groups. One generation's scoundrel may prove to be another's hero. Some genealogies report matters in relatively neutral terms, while others involve characterizations that reflect deeply held prejudices. No single perspective on a given nation in the book of Genesis should be taken as a steadfast historical principle held by all ancient Israelites at any given moment in history. To illustrate this point, let's consider a brief passage in Genesis 19, which provides a scathing parody of the origins of the Moabites and Ammonites. Toward the end of Genesis 19 (vv. 30–38), Lot's daughters seduce their father so as to become pregnant. The story unfolds as follows:

> "Let's make our father drink wine, and we will lie with him, so that we will live through the seed of our father." So they had their father drink wine that night, and the first-born daughter lay with her father, but he did not realize that she had either lain there or gotten up . . . [The next] night they also made their father drink wine, and the younger one went and lay with [Lot]; he didn't realized when she had either lain there or gotten up. Thus both of Lot's daughters became pregnant by their father. The first-born daughter bore

---

1. Genealogies in Genesis occur in the following chapters: all of 5; 6:9–10; all of 10; 11:10–32; 25: 1–18; all of 36.

a son and named him Moab; he is the father of the Moabites of today. And the younger also bore a son, and she called him Ben-ammi; he is the father of the Ammonites of today.[2]

What could be more insulting than to have your origins attributed to an act of drunken incest between a father and a daughter, schemed by the daughters, no less? Obviously, the author of this passage did not think well of the Moabites or the Ammonites (not to mention Lot himself). But this pejorative depiction of Moab was not shared by all. The genealogy at the end of the book of Ruth conveys a rather different attitude:

> So Boaz [the Israelite] married Ruth [the Moabite]; she became his wife, and he cohabited with her. The LORD let her become pregnant, and she bore a son. The women said to Naomi, "Blessed be the LORD, who has not withheld a redeemer from you today! May his name be perpetuated in Israel!" . . . The neighbors gave him a name: "A son is born to Naomi!" They named him Obed; he was the father of Jesse, father of David. (4:13, 17)

Hardly a more astounding contrast could be imagined. In the Genesis story, the Moabites emerge from the most debased of sexual pairings. In the book of Ruth, a Moabite woman conceives because of *God's intercession* and her progeny include Israel's *redeemer*, King David. That Ruth is not born a Jew hardly hampers her ability to bear Israel's future political and military savior.

We could point to a number of other biblical passages that parallel this odd contrast in attitudes toward a single nation. But let me here summarize what has been said thus far. First: identity contingent on distinguishing the "We" from "the Other" is rooted in genealogies, ostensibly because "blood" can be construed as an objective marker of identity. And second: any particular attitude regarding a specific nation found in one part of the Bible should not be taken as having been universally accepted in any given period or even over time.

Both of these facts tend to leave "We/They" identity politics rather contentious. This has not hindered an ongoing engagement with this approach; indeed, many Jews today still find these ideas to be powerful elements in their own sense of self. In his book *The Beginning of Jewishness*

---

2. This is my translation. Most published translations use softer idioms that neutralize the crassness of the event. For instance, JPS renders verse 36 as "both the daughters of Lot came to be with child by their father," but "with child" is to my ears quite a bit softer than the literal meaning, "pregnant by."

(1999), Shaye J. D. Cohen delineates how Jews were constantly revisiting the question *Who is a Jew?* because of changing historical circumstances. Perhaps the best-known adaptation in Jewish identity politics remains the shift from patrilineal to matrilineal descent (apparently) during the Roman Era. But while this is the best known, it is hardly the most profound adaptation.

More consequential would be the identity politics created by authors throughout our history who saw *the content of one's Judaism* as more important than any particular inherited trait. This approach to identity emerges from the Torah itself. At some very fundamental level, biblical writers *beyond the book of Genesis* recognized that blood lineage could never adequately establish the grounds for distinctiveness or allegiance. Some understood that distinctions between peoples who were originally next-of-kin (such as Ishmael and Isaac, or Jacob and Esau) were at best artificial. They recognized that the most significant elements of Jewish living—the cultural content and religious practices that constitute its distinctiveness—contribute to a form of self-definition that is superior to vague claims that *We* are simply *Other* than someone else.

This was not, however, an insight held by the authors of Genesis. The book of Genesis does nothing to foster the *content of Jewish identity* beyond clan association. The writers of other biblical passages (in the Torah and elsewhere) would take it as their task to remedy what they saw as Genesis's limited utility in the formation of Jewish identity. While they sustained aspects of "We/They" politics in their own writings, they ultimately transcended them with the laws, customs, ethics, and ideological positions that dominate their literary legacy.

The challenge of the book of Genesis for liberal Jews starts in that otherwise innocent-sounding genealogy of chapter 10. For there we have set in motion a cultural paradigm for self-differentiation that cannot, in my opinion, be sustained by those of us seeking a vibrant Judaism through cultural creativity and ongoing spiritual renewal. It is in our power to assert that no one is a Jew by historical fiat, but that all Jews are Jews by choice. This is the conviction held by the books of Exodus and Deuteronomy, and in the closing section of the book of Joshua. The covenant scenes in these books require that each individual affirm his or her allegiance; no individual is part of the covenant unless they have actively affirmed their commitment. In Exodus 24:7 we read: "[Moses] took the book of the covenant and read it aloud to the people. They responded, 'All that Yahweh has spoken we will do faithfully.'" Another covenant scene appears in the book of Joshua (24:22): "Joshua said to the people, 'You are witnesses regarding yourselves that you have willfully chosen to serve Yahweh.' The people replied, 'We are [free] witnesses.'" Such sentiments dominate the entire narrative of Deuteronomy, where being a Jew is about making a choice to choose life! These authors saw a covenant entered voluntarily as more powerful than any notion of birth-into-a-covenant. These passages undermine the notion of Jew-by-birth.

Too often, when the politics of identity are rehearsed in the modern world among Diaspora and Israeli Jews alike, this profound insight of Torah is subordinated for the sake of reactionary, shallow notions of clan. It is time for us to consider the meanings of our identity through free-will affirmations of commitment, rather than acquiesce to customary medieval, halakhic notions of *who is a Jew*, which violate the more profound insights of Torah.

Some might hold that birth into a Jewish family makes this choice easier to come by than for others. But given well-documented assimilationist trends, no one should assume that "ease" constitutes a significant factor in the creation and sustaining of a Jewish identity and life. Only identities that involve active choice lead to meaningful engagements with Jewish living. If we had only the book of Genesis, birth might constitute a sufficient criterion for establishing who is a Jew; but as it is, Torah transcends the mere sum of its parts. Meaning is created, not born. And so it is with each and every Jew. That I am taking direct aim at all theories of identity by descent—maternal or paternal—should be blatant enough. Reform Judaism should rethink its own politics of identity, and in the process, reaffirm its commitment to the more profound insights of Torah.

While the ideology of genealogically based identity may prove to be increasingly irrelevant to Reform Jews over time, this does not detract at all from the book of Genesis as a whole. The discrete stories in this book address many core concerns of the human condition beyond that of identity, including faith, justice, destiny, appeasement, dislocation, abandonment, and vulnerability. And these are the concerns with which we will be occupied in the following chapters.

4

Understanding Origins

A Survival Strategy

In one form or another, all ancient civilizations were typically defined by: (1) sojourn in a designated land; (2) a governance structure that was at once autonomous and indigenous; and (3) a religion organized around well-defined cultic sites, usually administered by a priestly guild or caste. The smaller "nations" of the ancient world were sooner or later swallowed up by larger conquering forces, leaving traces of their existence only in literature or buried beneath the sands of history for archaeologists to excavate. Israel should have been no exception. When Jerusalem fell to the Babylonians in 586 BCE, Israel should have ceased to exist like all other conquered peoples, given that each of the rubrics we just identified as typical of civilizations was undermined: a substantial portion of its people were exiled; its monarchy was eliminated; and its central and countryside cultic sites were destroyed, with its priests suffering the effects of displacement. Torah speaks of Jebusites and Amorites, Perizzites and Kenites, among many other "nations"; none of them can boast of a minute vestige in the world today. Of course, there are other ethnic groups that have managed to defy the dominant rules of history. However, they are very few in number and generally survived at the margins of civilization.[1] The Jews stand unique even among this rare cluster of survivors. They survived not one, but multiple conquests, and millennia of frequent persecutions. Differenti-

---

1. Commonly known are the Basque, who speak Euskara, a language whose roots are uncertain, and the Gypsies, who have preserved Romany, which scholars believe to derive from early Indian dialects.

ating them yet further is the *manner* in which they survived. This occurred not along the margins of civilizations, nor in remote regions of the world. Jews developed independent cultures while remaining engaged with the cultural and economic structures of their host societies.

What can account for this extraordinary feat in antiquity? The Jews developed an innovative cultural system that was able to sustain a people without those societal rubrics noted above: land, king, and fixed cultic sites. They replaced those standard rubrics with a most unlikely substitute: a literature and a method for disseminating its contents. This is to say, a cluster of words—Torah—was offered as a solution to the traumas of history. As preposterous as it might sound to suggest that *a literature* is what saved the Jewish people, I see no better explanation. My goal here is not to be gratuitously boosterish for Jewish survival, but to understand the dynamics of our survival, both initially, at the very moment in time that Judaism should have succumbed to the overwhelming forces of history, and then repeatedly throughout subsequent eras.

Survival was the focal point for those who composed Genesis. The Genesis writers recognized that stories of origination could foster a strong sense of ethnic identity. The past would serve as a foundation for the development of solidarity in the face of the chaotic circumstances of dispersion. Exile undermined everything stable in traditional cultures. The Torah in general, and the book of Genesis in particular, was created to counter that instability. It sought to nurture a sense of (collective) self that would transcend the traditional structures of place, leadership, and cult. Genesis—and by extension, Torah—is about survival.

In the aftermath of the conquest of the sixth century BCE, the architects of Torah chose three literary themes as rallying points for the formation of the Jews' consciousness in a transitional era: (1) the story of ancestors (Genesis); (2) the story of an exilic sojourn and redemption (Exodus); (3) the story of a prophet through whom God speaks (Deuteronomy). Each of these themes contributed to the development of an ethnic identity at a time when traditional notions of identity were under siege. And each of these stories is about *Israel in exile*. To understand the book of Genesis one must understand the circumstances that provoked its creation. Those circumstances are not part of the history of Abraham's era; rather, they derive from the contemporary affairs of the authors' own day. Abraham is not some real historical figure to whom the events of Genesis happened;

Abraham conveys the authorial voice as it struggles to lend meaning to the experiences of his own generation.

These three themes originally developed independently of one another. Different imaginations came up with different solutions. Eventually they were fused together into what is now Torah. This means that Genesis was just *one part* of a broader array of literary endeavors, each pursuing distinct approaches to the same issue: How do we create a sense of solidarity when everything we took to define ourselves is in a state of crisis? Our task here is to focus on how the Genesis authors participated in this project of cultural reinvention.

The stories we now have in Genesis were originally part of a narrative that included many more episodes. By dropping some elements and incorporating others, the redactors ended up with a narrative that lacked an intrinsic continuity. To create that continuity they sometimes built what might be called "narrative bridges." A prime example is the Joseph story, which quite literally *bridges* the experience of the patriarchs with the sojourn in Egypt. More pervasive is the integration of two ideological strands throughout the narrative. The first we already mentioned with regard to *the Noah Story*: the idea of genealogical continuity. The second emerges in Genesis 12–15: the idea of covenant between God and Abram's descendants. Through these strands—which together form what I have referred to as the "ideological overlay"—Genesis helps its audience develop a sense of self without the traditional social and political institutions intact. In effect, the Genesis author is saying to his audience: *If Abram could do it, we can do it!*

In Genesis 15 God's promise to Abram is elucidated in all of its parts. Abram will have a future of prosperity, progeny, and land ownership. These are the three components of the covenant *for the Genesis author*. Other authors envisioned the covenant differently. For instance, in the stories written by the author commonly referred to as the Deuteronomist, Israel's rights to its "ancestral lands" were contingent upon fulfillment of a rather detailed regimen of laws and social customs. That is, the covenant for the Deuteronomist was a bit different from that expressed in Genesis. His involved *commandments*. No such idea exists in Genesis.

There are many theories as to why shifts in the ideology of covenant took place, or why there may have been multiple approaches to covenant in a single generation. Unfortunately, we do not have the space to consider those theories here. Suffice to say, the authors of the three different allegorical approaches to Israel's past—ancestors, exile, and prophet—had distinct agendas in devising their particular approaches to covenant. However, it should be understood that the idea of a covenant with a deity was *not* unique to Israelites. All ancient civilizations saw their rulers as having been divinely "chosen," and this would have been true of Israel's monarchs as well. The difference that arises with Torah literature is that the covenant is no longer between a God and his chosen King, who then "represents" the people; the covenant is between God and the people directly, through an intermediary called a "prophet." This constitutes a radical departure from the ancient paradigms of covenant.

So on the one hand, Israel was like other nations in having the idea of "chosen-ness," but it was quite unlike the other nations in that it offered an approach to covenant that constituted a radical departure from traditional paradigms. This did not happen overnight. The Israelite idea underwent an evolution of its own, as I've already indicated when contrasting Genesis and Deuteronomy. However, like many conflicting images within Torah, the various ideologies of covenant did undergo some harmonization in the hands of the redactors who put the entire book together. So, for instance, when we get to the end of Deuteronomy (30:19–20), we read:

> I call upon heaven and earth today to bear witness: I have placed before you life and death, blessing and curse. Choose life so that you and your offspring might live, loving the LORD your God, heeding his voice, and holding fast to Him. For He is to be your life and assurance of longevity while dwelling upon the soil that the LORD swore to give to your ancestors, Abraham, Isaac, and Jacob.

One of the great inner tensions of Torah is that "the promise" of land, progeny and wealth articulated in Genesis is never realized in the stories of Abraham, Isaac, or Jacob. Consequently, the transition from Egypt to Canaan cannot be conceptualized as *a restoration*, for the land of Canaan had never been "Israel" at any previous point in the story. Thus, all the Deuteronomist could do was mention what had been sworn to the patriarchs, without giving too much detail as to the contents of that oath. The unsuspecting reader of Torah will do all of the harmonization required, perhaps never noticing just how much dissonance is injected by the forced fusion of a covenant based on commandments and a patriarchal covenant that had no such contingencies.

I want to emphasize that this dissonance is *literary, not historical*. People frequently confuse these things, and often abuse the text by misconstruing it as representing befuddled images of real life-events. The original book of Genesis likely ended with the fulfillment of the covenant as it is first presented in the Abraham narrative (Gen 12–15) and fulfilled with the birth of the twelve tribes living happily ever after in Canaan (Gen 30). Once the Torah redactors saw Genesis as a potential ancestral history *that led up to* the Egyptian sojourn story—written by a different author for different purposes—the dynamics of the *narrative* were permanently transformed. It was the process of integrating Genesis among the books of the Torah that resulted in "inconsistencies." When you take stories that originally have nothing to do with one another and force them into a sustained narrative, you are bound to end up with some rough edges. The ideological tension between the covenant-concept in Genesis and the idea of covenant in Deuteronomy is just such a "rough edge."

Were you to relate to the stories of Genesis and Exodus separately, as never having been fused into a single volume, just as you relate, say, to the story of Jonah and the book of Genesis separately, you would not think of them as "inconsistent." You would simply see them as two approaches to the same overwhelming problem: How can we transcend the chaos of dispersion? To give people hope, both stories demonstrate that Israel's ancestors had already survived dispersion—indeed, all of the formative episodes in the Torah take place *outside of the land of Israel.*

As noted, the writer of Deuteronomy integrated "remembrance" of the patriarchal covenant into his narrative. Yet other more aggressive steps were taken to harmonize the various strata of the literature. For instance, in Genesis 12–15, the editor added verses to the storyline that anticipate the integration of the Genesis and Exodus stories. In Genesis 15:13–17, he inserted an excuse for why the land would not be secured according to the surface meaning of God's promise during the era of the patriarchs. It reads as follows:

> **As the sun was setting**, a sleep-trance fell upon Abram, and a great dark dread overtook him. He [God] said to Abram, "Understand that your offspring shall be aliens in a land not their own, and they will be enslaved and oppressed four hundred years; but against the people whom they will serve, I will execute judgment, after which they will go free with great wealth. As for you, you will come back to your fathers in peace; you will be buried at a ripe old age. And the fourth generation will return here, for the guilt of the Amorites is not yet complete." **When the sun set** and it had become dark,

there appeared a smoke-oven, and a flaming torch, which passed
between those pieces.

The second of the two underlined phrases is what textual critics call a
"resumptive clause" (or *Wiederaufnahme*). It was common in antiquity to
emend texts, but there were various customs for accomplishing this. Frequently, when some kind of explanation or elucidation was added to a text,
the editor *resumed the narrative* after his insertion with an aspect of the
phrase that occurred just before his insertion. If you read Genesis 15 omit-
ting the verses presented here, you will find the story reads quite smoothly
and true to the dominant themes of Genesis.

Notice that the insertion here does not make direct mention of Egypt,
per se. Also notice that the duration of the sojourn is given as 400 years—a
vague "estimate" that would have been understood to mean "very many."
This figure will be adjusted in the actual Exodus narrative to the more specific duration of 430 years (see Exod 12:41). The vague references to an
enslavement in a strange land and its duration are meant to prepare the
reader for "history" beyond the book of Genesis, while also shifting one's
expectations with regard to this book's ending.

Now, I do not wish, in this context, to discuss the theological tensions
created by this particular anticipatory passage, which, in many respects,
are more troubling than the narrative dissonances it sought to resolve. (For
instance, why would God think to subject his people to so horrendous a
fate?) But I do wish to emphasize that all of these tensions emerge as a result
of the anthologizing process that created Torah. This compositional process
did not only result in tensions between stories that were originally distinct.
Sometimes, the original redactors chose stories because of their underlying
themes, but subsequent editors found something within them problematic,
and took it upon themselves to offer correctives. Two examples of this phenomenon can be drawn directly from the patriarch narratives in Genesis.

For one, consider that the very first story after the introduction of
Abram as a character (12:1–10) involves *removing* Abram and Sarai from
Canaan and placing them in Egypt (12:10–20). How does it make sense
to have the very first episode after arriving involve the *displacement* of the
protagonists from Israel? After all, the pretext for leaving Mesopotamia was
procurement of the land of Canaan. First, let's make clear that the Wife/
Sister story in 12:10–20 is a story about wealth acquisition. The covenant
involves three components: progeny, land, *and* wealth. Obviously, the redactors found this story valuable because it left Abram rather well off. Later

editors were not quite so sure of the redactors' choice. This story not only dislocates the protagonists from the Promised Land, but places them in Egypt. On the one hand, the redactors would want to reserve that kind of displacement for another story (Joseph), and on the other hand, they would want to avoid displacement altogether. So, instead of having the couple move to Egypt, the rewritten versions of this story in chapters 20 and 26 have the couple "visiting" Gerar, which ostensibly is still within "the land." Moreover, the subsequent versions of the story repair some of the thematic awkwardness of chapter 12 (Abram, after all, is portrayed as a liar in order to save his own skin). This is not the place to go through in detail the way chapters 20 and 26 revamp the original tale, but I've engaged this example to make abundantly clear that within the book of Genesis we find various voices in dialog with one another. Keep in mind that the anthological character of ancient literature motivated editors to emend and add materials, but not to *remove* materials that had already gained a certain stability within the literary tradition.

Similarly demonstrative of the book's anthological character are fragments of stories that hint at now-lost narratives. Consider the following verses taken from Genesis chapters 11 and 12 respectively:

> (11:31) Terah took his son Abram, his grandson Lot, the son of Haran, and his daughter-in-law Sarai, the wife of his son Abram, and they went together from Ur of the Chaldeans to the land of Canaan; but when they had come as far as Haran, they settled down there.

> (12:1) The LORD said to Abram, "Go from your native land and from your father's household to the land that I will show you."

According to the verse in Genesis 11, it was *Terah*, Abram's father, who left Ur of the Chaldeans for a distant land. How, then, shall we understand Genesis 12:1? Clearly it involves an added incentive—the gift of a land—and there is divine intercession, something not suggested with regard to Terah. By the time we get to chapter 15, where, as we noted, the covenant's components will be fully elucidated, the notion that it was Abram who left Ur rather than his father is well integrated into the narrative. There we read:

> I am the LORD your God who *brought you out of Ur of the Chaldeans* to give you this land as a possession (15:7).

Those well versed in the text of Exodus will hear echoes of this verse's verbiage in the Ten Commandments (Exod 20:2): "I am the LORD your God *who brought you out of the land of Egypt . . ."* In effect, we have the exact same literary trope, easily adapted for both stories, because at their core, both stories are vaguely about the same thing. At some point in our people's history, the idea emerged that all movement from a state of displacement to a state of rightful sojourn could only occur by divine will. As such, the revisers of Genesis, by using this very imagery, depicted the journey from ancient Ur as a kind of redemption, in some sense similar to the redemption from Egypt as developed by the authors of Deuteronomy and Exodus. Abram traveled from an exilic state in Ur (later called Babylonia) to the land of Canaan, and centuries later Israel, under Moses, journeyed from exile in Egypt to the Promised Land. The Torah's very foundations rest on this notion of displacement and journey.

The fact remains that most Jews living in the Diaspora do not feel they are "displaced" like Abram of old; nor do they feel as if they are dwelling in an exilic state allegorically equivalent to Egypt. Unbounded love and unequivocal support for the State of Israel has not translated into massive immigration since 1956. In what might strike some as an odd twist in interpretive history, I shall argue that Torah was written precisely for those in antiquity whose lives paralleled today's globally dispersed Jews. Torah was written to *re-create a people* for survival in Diaspora. With this understanding, our reading of the text proves radically different from more traditional approaches. And it is with this understanding that our comments on the passages to follow will be developed.

5

The Ethics of Our Stories

Genesis 18–19

Our discussion here will focus on the story of Sodom and Gomorrah. But before getting to the story itself, I wish to put a number of ideas in place. The primary goal of my discussion here is to show how, within biblical literature, one can find an idea and its opposite in two different passages. In fact, this is so often the case that one should be particularly cautious when trying to summarize what the Bible "says" about any particular notion. The case we will consider uses the Sodom and Gomorrah story as its base text, and then traverses the canon all the way to the book of Jonah to find a polemic against the ideology expressed by the Genesis authors.

Another idea I wish to explore is what is commonly referred to by literary critics as *ethical criticism*. The word "criticism" here is a generic term for any *critical approach* to literature; the word *ethics* should be self-explanatory. Put together, we are talking about the ethics of reading literature within a culture. Just what does that mean?

As a distinct concept related to literature, ethical criticism emerged in the wake of the university curriculum debates of the 1960s and 1970s. In his book *The Company We Keep: An Ethics of Fiction* (1988), Wayne C. Booth recalls how a member of the University of Chicago faculty, Paul Moses, protested the teaching of *Huckleberry Finn* in a required undergraduate humanities course. Booth's agenda was set by this 1962 debate. Professor Moses felt that use of Mark Twain's book as part of "the literary canon" constituted a tacit sanctioning of its depiction of "Negroes" in nineteenth-century rural America. At issue were both the overt and subliminal messages sent by Twain's classic. Professor Moses wanted his colleagues to consider what effect a given piece of literature has on the students when it is listed as required reading. He pushed people to reflect upon the influence their choices may have, and he charged that those who assign a given work are responsible for the potential impact of their assignments, whether or not the impact is intended.

A heated debate ensued. No one wanted to censor the teaching of any piece of literature. Even so, people recognized that by establishing a curriculum they were conveying something about the value of the works included, and of those excluded, as well. Was the curriculum exclusively meant to convey something about the literary or aesthetic aspects of a work, or should a work's ethical value factor into its inclusion or exclusion? This is no high-in-the-sky theoretical issue. Each of us confronts these ethical concerns when we think about what children should be exposed to at any given point in their development. As teachers and parents, we regularly censor works through our choices, even if that censorship is only meant to apply during the developmental period in a child's lifetime. Creating a course's "canon" is tantamount to expressing that some works have greater value than other works, at least in a given academic context. Shouldn't ethics be a significant criterion in that evaluative process?

There is yet another crucial ethical element involved in establishing the status of texts within a curriculum. Clearly, ancient sources are going to include ideas that we, today, consider reprehensible. For instance, the Bible explicitly accepts the existence of slavery; polygamy is a cultural norm; and the annihilation of indigenous cultures is portrayed as divinely sanctioned, even mandated. Today, we reject each of these practices as immoral. When we read biblical passages that support such things, it is not possible to remain neutral. As for the few examples I've cited, our rejection of these particular practices hardly seems controversial. But I've chosen examples that are not convtroversial. Questions regarding stories whose purposes or messages are ambiguous provide ethical challenges that are less easily resolved.

The book of Genesis includes more than its fair share of stories that raise ethical questions. There is the story about the cruel treatment of Hagar and Ishmael by Sarah, as Abraham looks on passively. There is the story of a deity who calls upon the patriarch Abraham to sacrifice his son on an altar—a passage that subjects both the father and the son to unimaginable psychological stresses. One could write extensively about the ethical implications of both of these scenes. I wish to turn our attention, however, to what I consider the even more complicated ethical problems raised by the Sodom and Gomorrah story. This story not only contains irresolvable indeterminacies, but its core message was so troubling as to inspire another biblical author to write a polemical counter-story.

In this Genesis story, even God recognizes that the plan to destroy Sodom and Gomorrah is morally questionable. He reflects, "Shall I obscure from Abraham what I am about to do?" (18:17). Given that Abraham is destined to instruct his descendants about what is "just and right" (v. 19), God figures he needs to justify his decision. This suggests that the authors of the story, while quite intent on the condemnation of these cities—here metonyms for a particular sort of people—are nonetheless aware of how the story's development reflects badly on their deity. They provide a rather muddled pretext: the sin of these cities is excessive, which implies that God has no alternative but to destroy them. But details remain sparse, and just how we are to understand *excessive* remains ambiguous. In fact, the lack of clarity leads to Abraham mounting a challenge to his deity. It is inconceivable that a city, even a city of predominantly evil people, is devoid of innocent individuals. Does the wickedness of even a majority outweigh the innocence of even a small minority? Abraham tests God's resolve by offering fifty innocent people as a number worthy of sparing the cities. Eventually Abraham gets God to concede to as low as ten: "'What if ten should be found there?' and [God] answered, 'I will not destroy, for the sake of the ten.'" That is the end of the discussion; God and Abraham part ways. Since the cities are destroyed, we are left to believe that ten innocents could not be found, even among children. Are we to imagine that there could ever be a circumstance in which children are so irredeemably evil as to warrant a death sentence? What are we to teach regarding the *meaning* of this story? Abraham asks God, "Shall not the judge of all the world execute justice?" (18:25). Given the conclusion of the story, the lesson would appear to be that the destruction of the city *was* justified. If we do not sustain that perspective, then we must assume a tacit critique of God's character—which, incidentally, he seems susceptible to, given his thoughts of concealing his plans at the beginning of the story.

The problem, of course, is that this story is part of our canon. Unlike debates over the academic canon, where people can include and exclude titles based on any number of criteria, we have inherited our canon as is, and it is not about to change. So we are, in fact, *forced* to read this story and to evaluate how we will use it. Personally speaking, I cannot resolve the ethical implications of this passage. What was the author trying to convey by portraying God as callous, or by showing Abraham's initial assertiveness give way to cowardice in not insisting that surely a single innocent child will be present? One might say that my sensitivities are too modern and anachronistically imposed upon the ancient writer's rather distinct approach to things. But I can quite readily find within biblical literature itself an author who very much shared my own sensitivities; in fact, so much so that he offered the ancient reader a strong alternate approach to that found in Genesis.

The book of Jonah involves an extended ethical critique of the themes of the Sodom and Gomorrah story. In Jonah, an Israelite prophet is sent to convince a people of a foreign (pagan) city that they should save themselves by altering their behavior. As in our Genesis story (18:20–21), the wickedness of the city's inhabitants had become known to God (Jonah 1:2). In Jonah, however, the prophet is told to proclaim before the city's dwellers that they will suffer a devastating destruction in forty days' time unless they repair their behaviors. Very few details are provided as to how Jonah's words are received, but the people of Nineveh simply respond with belief in God. "They proclaimed a fast, aristocrats and paupers alike put on sackcloth" (3:5). The king of Nineveh himself decrees, "Let everyone repent regarding his evil ways and from the wrongs of which he is guilty."

Here is a point-by-point comparison of these two stories:

PROPOSED DESTRUCTION OF A PAGAN CITY

- God tells Abraham of his plans to destroy two pagan cities, Sodom and Gomorrah, so that Abraham will be able to teach what is just and right.
- God tells Jonah of his plan to destroy a pagan city, Nineveh, as punishment for their unethical behavior. God wants Jonah to motivate the people to repent, so that his planned punishment will be unnecessary.

THE JEWS' REACTION

- Abraham senses such destruction is unjust, since there should be some cluster of innocent people present, however minimal. He argues God down to considering a mere ten inhabitants of Sodom and Gomorrah as worthy of saving the city.
- Jonah believes the city should simply be destroyed, so he attempts to flee from his assignment on the open seas. His action endangers the

innocent people on the boat with him. He has himself thrown overboard, ostensibly to bring about his death.

GOD'S ACTIONS

- Abraham's attempt to assuage God ends abruptly at ten. The author does not have him push God further to consider even one innocent person, *nor is repentance ever entertained as an option.* Abraham departs and the fate of the city is left as it was first planned.

- Jonah is miraculously retrieved from the ocean's depths by a fish and he is forced to appear in Nineveh to create the opportunity for repentance. He informs the people of their options.

STORY'S CONCLUSION

- The people of Sodom and Gomorrah continue in their iniquitous ways and the cities and all of their inhabitants are annihilated.

- The people of Nineveh go into mourning; public repentance on a mass scale takes place. The planned punishment is now unnecessary, so the city is spared.

Looming over both narratives are these questions: What is just punishment? Is repentance always acceptable? To what lengths should we go to avoid punishments that have irreversible effects? Justice in the Jonah story means *saving the people from their destiny.* Justice in the Abraham story means *punishing those who deserve punishment.* In Jonah, God stands for justice; in Genesis, Abraham appears to be the voice of justice, unless, of course, we accept the premise that Sodom and Gomorrah were fundamentally irredeemable (which is surely the attitude of the writer). In Jonah, God rebukes Jonah's insensitivity over the destruction of Nineveh: "Should I not care about Nineveh, that great city, in which there are more than a hundred and twenty thousand persons who do not yet know their right hand from their left, and many beasts as well?" The God in our Genesis story does not convey this type of sensitivity to animals, never mind people.

My purpose here is to highlight just how important it is to evaluate the ethical implications of all texts, whether they be canonical or not. Within Hebrew Scriptures one can very often find two stories that explore the very same underlying theme, but from opposite perspectives. This is why overarching attempts to teach *what the Bible says* are deeply flawed. Is the Genesis story's message more intrinsically *biblical* than the Jonah story's message? That is, should we focus primarily on the notion that there are intractable forms of moral turpitude that require the annihilation of an entire civilization, or are we supposed to rebuke the Jonahs of this world who hold that there are times when destruction is to be preferred over repentance?

These questions deserve to be the focal point of our religious reflection. They are the very questions that prompted an author to compose Jonah. The fact that this comparison between these stories is only rarely engaged has a great deal to do with how the Pentateuch's texts are privileged above passages found in the so-called prophetic books. Rather than accept a text's status as earned on the basis of something intrinsic to the text itself, we should recognize that the status of any given book has everything to do with the social forces that governed its reception at the moment of its publication, as well as the status it accumulates over time. But this leaves us with a moral conundrum not unlike that of Jonah's author. Just as that author would not call for the annihilation of Ninevah, he similarly did not call for the removal of the Genesis story. That is, the older story was left to stand, but his position was put in circulation to present an alternative approach. While authors long gone cannot be called upon to repent for their misjudgments, contemporary readers can be asked to develop sensitivities to the ethical implications of the act of reading. And that, I suppose, was the Jonah author's goal.

6

On the Permanence of Graves

Genesis 23

Burying one's dead: what could be a more fundamental rite? The scene in which Abraham buys a gravesite from a Hittite for Sarah is often commented upon for the highly stylized negotiation that results in the acquisition. Scholars relate to this material as a rare glimpse of social-business history. I wish to focus on something far more basic: the very notion that burial assumes land ownership.

We know very little about biblical-era traditions of burial or attitudes toward the dead. This led one scholar to call customs relevant to the ancient Israelite cult of the dead "a hidden heritage." In an article published in the 1970s, H. C. Brichto suggested that during the pre-Persian eras—that is, before 538 BCE—Jews were particularly concerned that family members be properly buried on ancestral lands. Since death was understood as a continuation of life, including retained memory, consciousness, and awareness of all that was happening with descendants, one's afterlife was to take place *where one belonged*—on clan-owned lands.[1] As Jews increasingly became citizens of the world—either through forced exiles or migrations—historical circumstances forced traditional attitudes toward the dead to be abandoned. Identity along clan and geographic lines diminished. With in-

---

1. H. C. Brichto, "Kin, Cult, Land and Afterlife—a Biblical Complex," *Hebrew Union College Annual* 44 (1973) 1–54. And see also Karel van der Toorn, *Family Religion in Babylonia, Syria, and Israel: Continuity and Change in the Forms of Religious Life*, Studies in the History and Culture of the Ancient Near East 7 (Leiden: Brill, 1996), especially chapter 9, "A Hidden Heritage."

creased urbanization in the land of Israel from the Persian period onward, identity had less to do with specific regions of land than it did with the place a family lived, whether or not it involved a historic association. A Jew living outside of the land of Israel might entertain burial in the Holy Land as an ideal, but such a burial more often than not proved unfeasible.

Consequently, the story of Abraham's acquisition of Machpelah, a burial cave, is packed with irony. Technically speaking, he is on the very land he has been promised, but he rightly identifies himself as "a resident alien," making clear that nothing truly belongs to him. Nothing of this land will belong to any Jew prior to the return of the Egyptian exiles many centuries after Abraham's lifetime. Thus, the authors of this particular story initiate the *ideal* of burial in the Holy Land. This ideal will be concretized through Jacob's burial, which involves transporting his bones back from Egypt, where he dies (Gen 47:30), to the land destined to become Israel. Even as this ideal is formulated, the reader cannot help but be impressed by the notion that *even* Abraham had to acquire a grave for his wife in a land that was not (yet) his own. In a very profound sense, then, Abraham had to behave like his many descendants who did not have access to ancestral property. The pattern he symbolizes would become the dominant pattern of Jewish life after the destruction of Jerusalem in 586 BCE.

The fact that Abraham refuses to take land offered him for free (23:6–9) stems from his desire to achieve a legally legitimate and irreversible hold over his parcel. The principle underlying this acquisition is very simple, but the social dynamic will prove harsh. No social or legal convention would guarantee Jews peace in their graves in subsequent eras. With its stone witnesses to the deceased and its tranquility, a gravesite is among the most stable of cultural symbols. And yet, "life in the grave" for the Jew has all too frequently been robbed of its most precious dignities. Once the Diaspora commenced, the experience of being denied the grave began. Much of our Bible conveys an awareness of the shift in fates for the living and the dead with the destruction of Jerusalem itself—the moment that defines the beginning of Diaspora. The book of Psalms records the devastation of Jerusalem, speaking of the corpses of God's servants strewn "as food for the fowl of heaven, and the flesh of Your faithful for the wild beasts. They have poured out their blood like water round about Jerusalem, and there was none to bury them" (79:2–3). The heartrending character of such narratives, whether they derive from antiquity or the Holocaust, lies in the many layers at which the violation of one's humanity is implied by such a scene. It is one thing to be killed; it is yet more horrible to imagine that one's death fails to be commemorated through ritual and burial.

A deep element of our humanity is expressed through how we relate to the deceased. Such rituals say less about the dead than they do about the living. The issue here is not whether burial is somehow more appropriate than, say, cremation, as a Hindu would practice it. The issue is how a culture exercises control over this very important structure for expressing the sanctity of life. Despite the fact that since the Hellenistic Era, Jews have held various beliefs about an afterlife, views about the grave itself remained unchanged: it needed to be permanently at peace, undisturbed, and with the remains of a corpse intact, waiting for the final resurrection. An afterlife was dependent upon the meritorious character of a person's life, and upon a peaceful existence in the grave.

Evidence regarding cemetery acquisition is rather spotty throughout ancient history. Frequently, local idiosyncrasies governed the character of transactions. In some parts of Europe and the Mediterranean, Jews could and did buy land outright for graveyards; in other places, land for cemeteries was granted as if on a lease, and Jews paid ongoing rent on the parcels. In other parts of Europe—Portugal, for one—Jews were forbidden altogether from establishing graveyards. Laws in medieval England were equally severe. Some Jews arrived in England as early as the late Roman period, but it was not until 1177 that they were granted cemeteries wherever they lived.[2] Until that time, all Jews on the island were buried in one London cemetery, regardless of where they were when they died. Jewish life in England was abruptly ended when King Edward I issued an edict of expulsion in 1290. Readmission only became permissible by law in 1656. There are consequently no remains of medieval Jewish cemeteries in England, as they were all taken over by local landowners or the Church, desecrated, and reverted to common usages.

Cemeteries were frequently moneymakers for the Church or other landholders in medieval Europe. In effect, the dead were tenants in perpetuity. Frequently called "Garden of the Jews" or "Mount of the Jews" in French medieval Latin records, cemeteries were only rarely owned outright by Jews of France after the seventh century. Even when they appear to have been actual "property," the massacres and expulsions that began with the

---

2. See Norman Golb, *The Jews in Medieval Normandy: A Social and Intellectual History* (Cambridge: Cambridge University Press, 1998) 7 n.9.

First Crusade in 1096 made the formal or legal status of cemetery owner-ship irrelevant.

The Jews were expelled from France in 1306 by King Philip "the Fair" as part of a plan to finance a variety of projects, including warfare. In the same year he issued a variety of edicts allowing for the auctioning off of all Jewish properties, "sold in perpetuity to the highest bidder." The charter for the Rouen auction stipulates that "houses, gardens, cemetery, lands, goods, possessions and all real estate whatsoever, which the Jews of Rouen possessed in the city of Rouen and its outskirts" were to be put on the auction block.[3] Needless to say, the edict also required that rather high auction fees and claims to rent owed on certain choice parcels were to be directed toward the king.

This "transference" of property was the norm in the wake of expulsions. Rarely was the cemetery treated any differently from other seized lands. In Erfurt where Jews enjoyed a vibrant cultural and economic sojourn in the early thirteenth century, the cemetery was leveled and transformed into a granary shortly after the expulsion of 1458. Recent excavations in Erfurt resulted in the discovery of Jewish gravestones throughout much of the old city, where they were used as pavers and as parts of retaining walls. Such circumstances were common throughout much of Europe.

There were many superstitions associated with disturbing the remains of the dead—Jewish or otherwise. Consequently, the reversion of cemetery lands into usable property after the expulsion of Jews presented something of a dilemma. To resolve this problem, desecration of Jewish cemeteries, along with the plundering of Jewish properties, became almost a ritual act. In Christian eyes, the reclaiming of Jewish burial grounds symbolized Christianity's victory over Judaism in life as well as in death. There are sto-ries of gravediggers who were reluctant to exhume what they knew, deep down, should not be disturbed. Wages, therefore, were inflated to motivate those charged with the task of discarding Jewish remains, while the work itself was deemed a victory celebration over the remains of "Old Israel."

The permanence that Abraham sought by acquiring his cave of Mach-pelah would be short-lived. Not only is the whereabouts of this cave un-known, but it remains for Diaspora Jews more a symbol of the insecurities of history than of a permanent resting place. My goal, however, in raising this approach to this story of "The Life of Sarah" in Genesis, is not to dwell

3. Ibid., 561.

on the lachrymose details of Jewish suffering even in the grave, but rather to look for a way to transcend the realities of history itself.

Dr. Susan Einbinder has written a powerful and moving scholarly history of Jewish martyrdom poetry in medieval France called *Beautiful Death*. She and other historians note that the bodies of Jewish martyrs—people who were publicly executed for refusing to convert to Christianity—were often abused and invariably discarded by the Christian executioners rather than being permitted honorable burials. This strategy would prevent Jews from establishing graves for martyrs, along with the rest of their potential symbolic meaning. Denied these burials, poetry emerged as an alternative approach to memorializing the lives of the persecuted. Laments, extended narratives, and highly stylized poetic renderings of the events and lives of the martyrs were all composed to affirm that which the Christian executioners hoped to thwart in denying graves to the dead. "Poetry as a living, musical, dramatic performance," writes Dr. Einbinder, "constituted a symbolic frame of reference in which central issues of Jewish identity were formulated."[4]

The literature, then, proved more permanent than any of the commemorative cemetery stones, a historical truth that has stood since antiquity. This very irony, that the all-too-ephemeral word could serve as the most permanent marker of a life, was somehow understood by the Torah writers themselves. Here we are, at least 2,400 years after they lived, and we rehearse their words, despite not knowing their identities or the location of their graves. And the same is true of every martyr whose life and death was captured in poetry. The word proves to be an everlasting mausoleum for remembrance.

A PERSONAL EPILOGUE

Some years ago, I started researching my own family origins in Germany. This brought me to the burial places of ancestors. Some of the names on stones from the eighteenth or early nineteenth centuries were no longer visible, or just barely so. Little was known of the person for whom one or another marker served as a remembrance. Contrary to what I had hoped, with each visit, standing among those many stones, I felt increasingly

4. Susan Einbinder, *Beautiful Death: Jewish Poetry and Martyrdom in Medieval France*, Jews, Christians, and Muslims from the Ancient to the Modern World (Princeton Princeton University Press, 2002) 171.

empty. I wondered: Did it matter that these were "relatives" since I knew nothing of them?

A visit to one particular cemetery proved pivotal, when I said Qaddish and placed a pebble upon a stele that turned out *not* to be that of an actual family member, but someone with the same family name. Between that silent stone and my search for a symbolic framework for remembering ancestors that could contribute to our identity as Jews and as a family, there grew a tension. I found myself relating to those poems and narratives discussed in Dr. Einbinder's book as far more profound and effective than any fading obelisk situated in the ground on the other side of the globe. But they, of course, were highly charged, dramatic renderings, dedicated to recording the plight of those who were victims of history's most traumatic forces. Most of those I wanted to be memorialized were common people, ancestors certainly, but probably not extraordinary in any particular fashion. I began searching for a contemporary medium to achieve my goals.

Such a medium presented itself one day when I was flipping through an old family photo album. Many of the images were fading. To prevent them from being lost, I started digitizing photographs and restoring them. Some images dated back to the late 1860s. I began writing brief narratives for each image, drawing upon remembrances of older family members and various documents at my disposal. But I wanted to learn more. Doing further research, I discovered that many more members of my family were registered in the databases of Yad Vashem than we had realized. The place and date of their deaths—and tragically, the circumstances—were made known to the present generation for the first time. For those family members, my task grew particularly urgent. I felt that if I did not do this work, my own children would have no recourse to this family history, and no personal connection to this historical tragedy. The research led to birth records and, using the Internet, I was able to write to small towns in Switzerland and France and Germany to learn about emigration dates, jobs held, even apartments rented.

Slowly the photographs are being digitized and brief transcripts attached to each and every one. They exist on a website as clusters of zeroes and ones—in some sense, perishable with the flick of a switch, and yet more permanent than any stone could ever hope to be.

Most likely, Jews of the Diaspora will emulate Abraham for millennia to come, buying gravesites for their beloved with the hope of creating a permanent and tranquil resting place. But if history teaches us anything, it is that graves provide a false sense of stability. It may not be an expulsion that denies the next generation access to its deceased, but the mobility that dominates our era, where families are dispersed thousands of miles from where they spent their childhood, and from where they bury their dead. If we are to find meaning in remembering, if we are to create identity through connections with the past, it will be incumbent upon us as individuals and communities to create dynamic vehicles for remembrances. For the time being, the most permanent medium is made up of bits and bytes. And while in the medieval world, the creation of a lament or a poem of remembrance required a scribe with rarified skills and knowledge, today, the ability to create "a symbolic frame of reference" for future generations is in the hands of every computer-literate individual.

7

Recognizing Torah Voices

Genesis 27

Among the most exquisite stories in all of Tanakh is Isaac's blessing of Jacob. In this essay I wish to highlight the artistry of this author. I shall also draw attention to the bracketing structure that the redactor has built around the story. Finally, we will once again draw attention to how the Genesis author was attuned to the travails of Jewish life in the Diaspora. But first to the artistry.

If we ignore the *aesthetics* of our literature we fail to notice that some stories are written better than others. Why would this be important? Attention to aesthetics helps us discern the distinct styles and techniques of various biblical writers. In making this discernment, we also highlight the anthological character of the literature. Some authors wrote with a very direct style, with no ear for subtlety or intricate plot development. Others readily engaged ironic flourishes, allegorical imagery, and even humor. Many of the stories that exhibit somewhat compromised aesthetics probably started out quite a bit better than they currently read. One suspects that they have suffered from the integration of ideological materials that compromise their original literary integrity. An example of a compromised story occurs in Genesis 29:10–19. The first three verses of the story work wonderfully, as Jacob views a remarkable stairway to heaven. But then, suddenly in verse 13, the redactor has God standing next to Jacob on earth—which makes the stairway itself at best, incidental, at worst, irrelevant—and then he throws at us the standard ideological overlay of the covenant's threefold promise of land, progeny, and wealth. What, then, was the purpose of the stairway?

Angels frequently appear to patriarchs and others in biblical stories. Surely this "stairway" image had some other purpose in its original setting. By verse 16 Jacob awakes and nothing more is learned of what we sense was a scene displaced by the stereotypical ideological overlay in verses 13–15.

Perhaps you are wondering how we can go about making such judgments, since aesthetics are most often thought of as a matter of personal taste. Judging whether you like something is, indeed, a matter of personal taste. But in performing an analysis of a piece of literature, we can set up evaluative criteria that involve more or less objective assessments based on an internal evaluation of the literature's own characteristics. The ideological overlay we have referenced is just such a criterion. It is always external to a narrative's plot. Sometimes it is skillfully integrated, other times it is just sort of thrown in so that the redactor can repeat his primary concern. (One might argue that the example in Genesis 29:10–19 was *skillfully* executed since the story itself still seems to work.) As far as literary techniques go, we have an array of questions we can ask that concern the aesthetic characteristics of a narrative. For instance, does a story involve irony? Does a story involve word-play? Does a story pivot off of imagery that was set up in a previous narrative? Does a story pivot off of multiple layers of meaning? Throughout the Hebrew Bible we find the use of irony and word-play, and now and again we are quite struck by how a story functions at multiple levels—not simply because we think it does (subjectively), but because other biblical authors engage the multivalence of another narrative in their own stories. With this in mind, we can evaluate any given story by engaging at least some of the measures biblical authors themselves engaged. Now it may be that we won't agree on how skillful a particular author was in engaging these various literary techniques. Such disagreements will usually happen on the margins of what makes something ironic, or a word-play, etc. For the most part, these literary techniques are not all that subtle and the majority of us will at least agree on their presence, regardless of how we assess their qualities.

Aesthetic sensitivity also alerts us to the social context in which this literature was created. That is, its *beauty* is part of its entertainment value. And we should not for a second lose cognizance of this literature's function as entertainment. If the stories were not good, if they were not well crafted, they would not have attracted a loyal following in their original forms. As a whole, stories included in the anthology had to be sufficiently pleasing or challenging to survive, and then to warrant inclusion.

By engaging the text in terms of its aesthetic characteristics, we also hope to establish something about the history of its composition. As noted, some stories simply appear to be truer to their original aesthetic forms than other stories. Those stories whose aesthetic integrity has been compromised have almost invariably suffered from the workings of an aggressive redactor's pen—a redactor who had ideology high and aesthetics low on his list of values. Our discussion of Genesis 27 will show both forces at work.

I will provide here my own translation of the chapter's first 27 verses. I am deleting, for the time being, verse 23—a deletion I will explain below.

Isaac had grown old and he was losing his eyesight. He called to Esau, his eldest son: "Son!" He replied, "Yes." [2]"I'm an old man now. I don't know when I'll die. [3] You, take your gear, your quiver and bow, go out into the meadows and hunt for me some game. [4] Then prepare my favorite dish; bring it to me and I will eat, whereupon I shall bless you through my life before I die.

[5] Rebekah had been eavesdropping when Isaac was speaking with Esau his son. When Esau left for the meadows to hunt game to bring back, [6] Rebekah told her son Jacob as follows: "Look, I overheard your father speaking with Esau, your brother, saying, 'Bring me game and prepare my favorite dish and I will eat, and then I will bless you in the presence of Yahweh, before I die.' [8] Now, my son, listen to what I say, exactly what I command you: [9] Go out to the flocks and take from there two fine kids. I'll make them into your father's favorite dish, just as he likes it. [10] You will then serve it to your father and he will eat, whereupon he will bless you before he dies." [11] Jacob said to Rebekah, his mother, "But Esau, my brother, is a hairy man, and I'm smooth-skinned. [12] Perhaps father will touch me and I'll be thought of by him as a trickster. He will provide me with a curse rather than a blessing." [13] His mother replied to him, "Your curse would be upon me, my son. Just listen to what I've said and get them for me." [14] He got them and brought them to his mother, who made them into his father's favorite dish. [15] Rebekah then took the most precious clothes in the house belonging to her eldest son, Esau, and she dressed her younger son in them. [16] She then placed goat skins on his hands and upon the nape of his neck. [17] She handed him the prepared dish and bread she had made. [18] He went to his father. "Father." (Isaac) replied: "Yes, which son are you?" [19] Jacob replied to his father, "I am Esau, your first born. I've done as you asked me to do. Come now, eat of my game so that you might bless me through your life." [20] Isaac said to his son,

"Amazing how quickly you found [game], my son." He replied, "Yahweh, your God, caused it to be so for me." [21] Isaac said to Jacob, "Come close to me that I might touch you, my son, so that I might know whether you really are Esau or not." [22] Jacob approach Isaac, his father, and he touched him, and said to himself, "The voice is the voice of Jacob, but the hands are the hands of Esau."[1] . . . [24] He then said, "You are my son Esau?" He replied, "I am." [25] So he responded, "Well then, serve me, I'll eat of my son's game so that I might bless you through my life." He served him; he ate, he served wine, he drank. [26] Isaac, his father, then said to him, "Come to me and kiss me, my son." [27] He went up to him and kissed him and he inhaled the scent of his clothing, and he blessed him, saying, "Ah, the scent of my son is like the scent of the meadows that Yahweh has blessed."

Five times in this narrative Isaac questions who is standing before him (vv. 18, 20, 21, 24, 26). This makes altogether clear that the entire story pivots off of Jacob's *inability to trick his father*. But the author leaves this all quite subtle, and given Isaac's response to Esau later in the chapter (v. 35), one might believe that Isaac is a victim rather than a co-conspirator. The climax of Isaac's alleged uncertainty as to his server's identity is expressed in that glorious verse, "The voice is the voice of Jacob, the hands are the hands of Esau." Logic demands that Esau would not appear before his father using his brother's voice (as if that could be feigned anyway); nor is the substitute meal of domestic sheep sensible when game is expected. These verses, then, do not signal confusion on Isaac's part; rather, through them, the story-teller suggests the character's awareness. Isaac knows full well who is before him, and he transfers the responsibility for his complicit behavior to God himself when he calls for the most intimate and telling of tests—a kiss. The two men, face to face, cannot fool one another, but Isaac thinks to himself, "Ah, the scent of my son is like the scent of the meadows that *Yahweh has blessed*" (v. 27). The author construes the episode as engineered by Yahweh, Israel's God. As Isaac sees it, Yahweh is sending Jacob. After all, Isaac is also a man of the meadow and not a hunter (see 26:12) and in this way, Jacob is meant to be his successor.

The verse I left out of the story occurs right after that phrase about the voice being that of Jacob and the hands ostensibly being those of Esau. At that moment, the text adds the following comment: "He did not recognize him because his hands were hairy like those of his brother Esau; and so

1. Verse 23 has been deleted. It will be "restored" and discussed below.

he blessed him." This is a rather clumsy insertion executed by some editor who simply could not suffer the heightened ambiguity and subtlety that functions throughout this narrative. Whoever added this verse wanted to reframe the story so that the reader would be certain that Isaac was *not* complicit in the undermining of his eldest son's birthright. But as I pointed out a moment ago, the phrase about the voice and hands is not an admission of confusion, but a statement regarding Isaac's certainty. Moreover, the out-of-place character of this inserted verse becomes evident when one notes how it jumps to the blessing itself, despite the fact that there remain two more challenges to the server's identity before the blessing is to be conveyed (v. 24, just before the substitute meal is served, and v. 26, the kiss). Having read the story as rendered above without v. 23, if you now go back and re-read that section with the verse in place, you will quite readily sense how clumsily it disturbs both the flow and the plot of the narrative.

Isaac's blessing of Jacob, then, is a glorious, freestanding story that ended up in this anthology of stories for one main purpose: to move Jacob back to Paddan-aram. Esau's desire for vengeance, which is expressed in the passage following the verses offered above, is ostensibly the basis for Jacob's displacement out of harm's way. But the redactor integrated this rather straightforward element in the plot line with a more pressing religious concern: intermarriage. Our story in chapter 27 is framed by two thematically linked verses: 26:34 and 27:46. They read as follows:

> When Esau was forty years old, he took as a wife Yehudit, daughter of Beeri the Hittite, and Basmat, daughter of Elon the Hittite; and they were a source of bitterness to Isaac and Rebekah. (26:34)

> Rebekah said to Isaac, "I can't stand life because of the Hittite women. Were Jacob to marry Hittite women like these, local girls, what reason would I have to live?" (27:46)

With the addition of these verses, we now have two pretexts for Jacob's relocation to Paddan-aram: Esau's desire to kill Jacob—which emerges from the story of the absconded blessing itself and Rebekah's desire to find her favorite son a nice Jewish girl, a theme that is extrinsic to the blessing story of Genesis 27, and which was likely included by the same redactional hand that inserted verse 23 into the body of the story. The relocation of Jacob will result in his marriage to Leah and Rachel, neither of whom would qualify as "Jewish" according to the standards pursued by rabbinic Judaism after the Roman era. But endogamy—marriage within the clan—was the cultural concern of this biblical author.[2]

The Jewish mother's proclivity for melodrama proves to be a stereotype of considerable antiquity. Of course, it is an unequivocally negative image, but we can recognize that the male author is using the female's voice to cloak but still express his own intense emotionality on the subject. Just as Rebekah frames intermarriage as rendering *her* life meaningless, the notion that a son might be lost through intermarriage will ring clairvoyant for all future generations of Jews living in the Diaspora—not just for mothers, but for fathers alike. Once again, we see how attuned our Genesis story is to life of an exilic culture.

Admittedly, it is not easy to reconceptualize the Torah as a book focused on Diaspora living, especially after a lifetime of reading it as having been written *in the land of Israel* and *for the land of Israel*. But by this point in our essays on these stories, our case should already begin to stand on solid ground (see the Introduction). Esau, Jacob's brother, will inherit a land and remain there; but Esau is not a patriarch of Israel. Jacob will seek a wife in Mesopotamia, come back to make peace with Esau, but almost immediately thereafter find his entire entourage displaced to Egypt. When you are living in your own land, isolated from other cultures, you have no fears of intermarriage. The repeated retreats to Mesopotamia for wife-hunting, and the constant frustration of displacement—despite the covenantal promise—speak most loudly to those who were experiencing the very same tensions in real time: the Jews of the Diaspora.

In a way, that single verse about hands and voice tell the story of Torah itself. The hands are the hands of the land; the voice is the voice of the dispersed yearning for the land. Like Isaac, we should not be fooled. That voice cannot be disguised.

---

2. See the extensive comments on endogamy in chapter 4 above.

8

Our (More Or Less) Four Matriarchs

Genesis 28–31

From chapters 28 through 31 we are provided an array of stories that result in the creation of a people as a confederacy of tribes. One might expect a people's legend of origins to derive from events valorous or noble. None of this is true of the biblical depiction of Israel's derivation from three patriarchs who manifest neither nobility nor valor. We do not really know much about an actual ancient confederacy of tribes called "Israel" that would have coalesced prior to the book of Exodus's Egyptian sojourn. While I think it reasonable to assume there was just such a cluster of clans, the name "Israel" itself, as a designation for those people who would become *the Jews*, was probably a late arrival on the historical scene.[1] The Jews who descended from those people occupying the regions later labeled Israel (or Samaria) and Judah would eventually call themselves either *Yisrael* or *'Ivrim* (Hebrews). But unfortunately, there are no sources outside of the Hebrew Bible that attest to the character of this confederacy either before,

1. The earliest inscription bearing the name "Israel" is the Merneptah Stele, dated to c. 1208 BCE. This includes just the word and an obscure reference to "destroying the seed." Some scholars read the hieroglyph as meaning "Jezreel" rather than "Israel," but even if we take the inscription to mean the latter, the late thirteenth-century date would place this mention some 400 to 500 years after what would ostensibly have been the "Patriarchal Era" discussed in this essay (that hypothetical date derived from the internal chronology of the biblical narrative itself, based on the number of generations between Abraham and Moses). However one takes the significance of the Merneptah inscription, no information derived from that stele influences our consideration of the material at hand.

during, or after the period of the monarchs (which lasted from the tenth century until 722 BCE in the north, and until 586 BCE in the south). No matter how you date the sources of our Hebrew Bible—that is, whether you say they come from the tenth century or the fifth century BCE—nothing on record would date from within 500 years of the "patriarchal/matriarchal" era. Consequently, we have every reason to read our Genesis story of the tribal origins of ancient Israel as a form of *memory construction*. By that I mean the writers wanted to create a collective memory for the sake of fostering a sense of ethnic unity. The collecting of the stories that make up these particular chapters regarding Jacob's four wives likely took place after Israel had experienced the Babylonian Exile. Whether they actually stem from more ancient local traditions can be neither proved nor disproved.

Part of the complexity of our narrative has to do with achieving twelve tribes. Why twelve? This was a standard trope in antiquity, perhaps derived from some actual historical circumstances, or perhaps just an idealized notion. The great Delphic Amphictyony of ancient Greece—an amphictyony being a confederacy established to protect a shared interest—was ostensibly a league of twelve tribes when it was founded (in later years it expanded to include more than twelve). There is some evidence that a preference for having twelve constituents form a significant unit dates back to ancient Sumer (early second millennium BCE). Documents from ancient Nippur suggest that the cultic center celebrated its two primary national deities, Enlil and Ninlil, as well as ten regional deities—bringing us to a total of twelve gods.[2] In the Bible, Ishmael, like Jacob, is the "father of twelve chieftains" (Genesis 17:20 and 25:16). When the scribe Ezra wants to set up an assembly of priests, he creates a panel of twelve (Ezra 8:24). As we will see, the insistence on achieving twelve tribes cannot reflect some actual historical circumstance because Jacob simply did not have twelve sons who formed twelve tribes. Consequently, twelve appears to be the ideal the redactor was aiming at, and the stories, which do not exactly accommodate twelve tribes, were forced to fit the mold.

Just how was that accomplished? The twelve sons of Jacob, according to Genesis 31 and 35 are recorded as follows:

Reuben, Simon, Levi, Judah, all born to Leah

Dan, Naphtali, born to Rachel's surrogate, Bilhah

2. See William W. Hallo, "A Sumerian Amphictyony," *Journal of Cuneiform Studies* 14.3 (1960) 88–114.

Gad, Asher, born to Leah's surrogate, Zilpah

Issachar, Zebulun, born to Leah upon her becoming fertile again

Joseph, Benjamin (only recorded in 35:18), born to Rachel

Now this is a very curious list. Six of the twelve sons are born to Jacob's wife, Leah, who became his wife as a result of Laban's trickery and his apparent inability to discern the beautiful Rachel from her homely elder sister in bed on his wedding night. Four of the tribes derive from women who are designated "surrogate mothers" rather than full wives. In antiquity, it was not uncommon for a woman from a family of means to be married with a concubine who would potentially serve as a surrogate in the event she proved infertile. The child of that surrogate counted as the full wife's own. We saw this pattern with Sarah and Hagar. The ancient collections of laws known as Ur-Nammu (circa 2000 BCE) and Ammurapi (or Hammurabi, circa 1750 BCE) provide us with evidence of surrogacy practices. One law indicates that if a wife has not given birth within two years of marriage, she is required to provide a slave girl for the husband. The child will remain with the original wife and she may "sell [the surrogate] wherever she pleases." In another document we learn of a slave girl who, having borne a child, suddenly "goes about making herself equal to her mistress." In this particular case, the mistress is not permitted to sell her, but "she may put a slave mark on her and count her among the slaves."[3] Apparently, wives in some contexts were within their rights to banish surrogates, citing insolence or some other intolerable behavior as the pretext; other contexts did not permit banishment, but did permit a permanent mark of servitude.

Ostensibly, a surrogate is only to be engaged when a woman has proven barren, but this is obviously not the case with Leah. She has borne four sons already. Only after experiencing a cessation of pregnancies (one that will prove temporary) does she hand over her surrogate, Zilpah, to Jacob (30:9–13). From a legal standpoint, there is no way to make sense of this, and one can only assume that the author's audience would have been just as aware of this irregularity in practice as we are.

Ironically, Leah is subsequently blessed with the resumption of her fertility, after a most bizarre scene. Leah *buys* a night in bed with Jacob as a result of Rachel's quest to purchase certain fruits (usually rendered "mandrakes") harvested by Leah's son, Reuben (30:14–21). The Hebrew for

---

3. These cases are presented in Matitiahu Tsevat's essay "Hagar and the Birth of Ishmael," in *The Meaning of the Book of Job and Other Biblical Studies: Essays on the Literature and Religion of the Hebrew Bible* (New York: Ktav, 1980) 70–72.

"mandrakes" is *duda'im*, whose root shares letters with a word for "love," a fact that has led some to suggest that the fruit may have been considered an aphrodisiac, or perhaps even a magical fertility drug. This might explain the barren Rachel's motivation in acquiring them. Only, the irony is all too clear: Rachel is dependent upon her rival Leah's son for this fertility drug, and Leah is dependent upon Rachel for acquiring intimacy in the bed of her husband Jacob. Upon getting Rachel to concede to her price, Leah confronts Jacob, saying, "You are to sleep with me, for I have *hired you* with my son's mandrakes." Apparently God is pleased by this scene and blesses Leah with renewed fertility: she bears two more sons, Issachar and Zebulun (as well as a daughter, Dinah). Just what the authors intended by including this brief scene amidst an otherwise dry genealogy cannot be said for certain. The assertiveness of this female character, while not altogether atypical of Genesis women (remember Rebekah!) might strike many a reader as an odd role reversal in antiquity, especially in matters related to sexuality. After all, the woman is *buying the man* (*sakhor sakhartikha*) for an evening dalliance, and the pun is driven home through the naming of her poor, unsuspecting son, *Issachar*—a play on "I will buy [him]." Rachel does, finally, become pregnant—after already having acquired Dan and Naphtali through her surrogate, Bilhah—and Joseph is born. Oddly enough, the birth of Benjamin is not recorded here. Rather, it appears as an afterthought in chapter 35, which also records Rachel's death in childbirth.

There are many elements we cannot fully explain or appreciate because we are missing key components of the cultural repertoire that were shared by the author and his intended audience. For instance, a significant component of the Israelite covenant with God is progeny. How, then, are we to understand this story, which treats the births of Jacob's children with dark humor, sarcasm, and considerable irreverence toward the majority of Israelite tribes. After all, it cannot be much of an honor to trace your lineage to the second- and third-tier cohabitants of Jacob—Leah, the undesired wife, and Bilhah and Zilpah, the standby surrogates. (Note, both Bilhah and Zilpah are referred to as "wives" in the introduction to the Joseph story (37:2) a kind of editorial "repair" of their status.) Yet that is precisely the circumstance for ten of the twelve brothers. Equally curious is the fact that the favorite wife, Rachel, produces only Joseph and Benjamin. The former does not engender a tribe at all. Instead, his two sons, Ephraim and Manasseh, are destined to take his place.

When we drop Joseph from the twelve and put his two sons in his stead, we end up with thirteen rather than twelve tribes. Clearly, adjustments had to be made. Reuben, Jacob's firstborn, is sometimes excluded from those defined as heirs, as is explained in 1 Chronicles 5:1. There we read that Reuben "defiled his father's bed" by seducing Bilhah, Jacob's (former) concubine—an episode that is recorded in one verse in Genesis (35:22). When Jacob offers blessings to his sons, his condemnation of Reuben is unequivocal: "Unstable as water, you shall excel no longer; for when you mounted your father's bed, you brought disgrace—my couch he mounted!" Consequently, his birthright is ostensibly passed on to Joseph's sons. It is one thing to have committed an immoral act, thus excluding one from an inheritance; it is yet another thing not to have actually constituted a "tribe" in real life. They don't seem mutually exclusive.

But even with Reuben out, the numbers still do not work perfectly. The book of Joshua insists that land assignments were by lot, which implies that no region was intrinsically associated with any historical tribal entity. The Levites, as priests, receive no land at all, so without them and without Reuben, we are back down to eleven. Later on in the book of Joshua, Reuben's descendants reappear as possessors of land (Joshua 18:7), receiving an inheritance alongside the descendants of Gad, Reuben's half-brother.

What are we to make of all this? Clearly, many of the underlying meanings of this story of origins have been lost to us amidst the cacophony of centuries of interpretation. This is not the place to concentrate on the contents of Jacob's blessing in chapter 49, but what is clear is that there were many folk legends operating under the surface here, most of which have left few remnants beyond the cursory images we capture in Genesis, Joshua, and Judges. Too many questions remain to be answered before we can even begin to speculate as to the passage's underlying message. But I think it fair to say that the authors of this narrative are playing havoc with birth imagery and the notion of tribal unity along simple birth-lines. Perhaps this reflected the reality of their own era, which saw tribal identity rendered largely irrelevant in the Diaspora, where land and clan could no longer be associated one with the other. Actual data for establishing the distribution of population in ancient Israel, either before or after the exile, are altogether lacking. Thus, whether there were clearly defined tribal regions along the lines stipulated in Torah cannot be ascertained through independent evidence. However, biblical literature hints at various cultural shifts that usually accompany increased urbanization. For instance, the Prophet Elijah is referred to as *Eliyahu Ha-Tishbi*—Elijah of the town of Tishbi, that is, a resident of Gilead (1 Kings 17:1). His clan membership is never mentioned.

By the time we get to the second century, the heroes of the Maccabean Revolt are the *Hasmoneans*. Both names, "Maccabee" and "Hasmonean" are of uncertain origins, but neither are traditional tribal designations. Perhaps these cultural shifts away from regionalism and tribalism are what enabled the biblical writers to look back upon legends of tribal origins with a carefully measured dose of sarcasm.

Much of our interpretive dilemma emerges as a result of a clash between the redactor's agenda and the story's original literary setting. In other words, the goals of the story's original author, who wrote for some setting now lost to us, were not exactly those of the person who placed this story in the anthology of legends we now call *Genesis*. That person, the redactor, sought to tell the story of Israel's origins using well-known characters and themes. But the story of Jacob, while serving most of his agenda quite well, would not work as a perfect fit. After all, the story he seeks to tell is about the origins of *Israel*, but no character in any of his narratives bears that name from birth. Jacob only becomes Israel through an ingenious change-of-name story (chapter 32), a technique already employed by the Genesis redactor with regard to the first patriarch and matriarch, Abram and Sarai. It is all too easy to read through these thematic dissonances with the redactor's harmonic intentions seen as dominant. But once one becomes attuned to the offstage voices, a far more complex literary history emerges than the one the redactor thought we would recognize. With that recognition we begin to understand what it means to become a people *through* literature.

9

A People by Any Other Name

Genesis 32–33

Toward the end of chapter 8, I noted that the collator of the Genesis stories had before him a real challenge: How could he take this cluster of ancestral legends about Abraham, Isaac, and Jacob, and end up with a people called *Yisrael*? In chapters 32 and 33 this problem is solved with remarkable literary ingenuity. The core story involves Jacob confronting Esau more than twenty years after absconding with the blessing Esau was to receive from Isaac. We, the readers—and Jacob, the character—expect Esau to kill his twin brother upon meeting him. In preparing for the meeting, Jacob divides his camp into two parts, a strategy he hopes will allow at least one cluster of his progeny to survive a confrontation with Esau's retinue. On the night before their encounter, Jacob remains alone by the edge of the river where they crossed into Canaan. There he encounters a "man" [*'ish*]. I'm going to render here a brief passage in chapter 32, which is drawn from a core motif that also appears in a story in the book of Judges:

> Jacob remained alone. A man struggled with him until dawn. He realized that he could not overpower him, so he struck at his hip-joint, dislocating it during the struggle. [The man] said, "Let me go, for dawn has arrived!" [Jacob replied], "I will not let you go until you bless me." He asked him, "What then is your name?" "Jacob." He said, "You shall no longer be called Jacob, but rather *Yisrael*, because you have struggled [*sariyta*] with gods and with men and prevailed." Jacob said, "Tell me your name." [The man]

replied, "What do you mean by asking for my name?" He then blessed him.

This is the core element of the story, adopted by the redactor from either another piece of literature or a widely known motif within the culture, as I shall demonstrate below. At the very moment in our narrative that Jacob is supposed to confront Esau in battle, he is instead portrayed as fighting with an unnamed man. This is what makes Jacob's inquiry as to his identity so very compelling. Twenty years have passed since the brothers have seen one another. Would they recognize each other in the dark of night? Should Jacob not assume that his attacker is, indeed, Esau? Whom else would he expect to attack him at this place and at this time?

There are a number of difficult idioms in this passage and various translations have offered an array of renderings. For instance, after Jacob says, "Tell me your name," the text has the unknown man reply, *lamah zeh tishal lishmi* which is rendered by the Jewish Publication Society translation (JPS 1985), "You must not ask my name!" (Gen 32:30). The Revised Standard Version (RSV, 1962, v.32:29) reads, "Why is it that you ask my name?" Note, JPS simply has him make a statement, and RSV makes the phrase into a question. I have written, "What do you mean by asking for my name?" by which I'm hoping to convey that the character is challenging Jacob, as he finds his question either insolent or ignorant (that is, he *should* recognize him—why doesn't he?). But I cannot be certain my rendering is any better than the other two. In a moment we'll see how the very same phrase is engaged in Judges, but even with the two instances together, the exact intent remains ambiguous.

In seeking the name of this night adversary, Jacob is mimicking his own father's question as to who it was who brought him food for a blessing. And just as was the case then, Jacob once again seeks a blessing. Only the circumstances are quite different. If this is, indeed, Esau, he will actually have fought with his brother and prevailed, thereby wrestling for the very blessing he previously absconded. The writer has built into the narrative an array of ambiguities so as to leave the reader guessing, but the artistry is uncompromised by these highly calculated indeterminacies. The attentive reader will recognize the echoing of motifs from his cultural repertoire, but here used ingeniously to transform a simple man, Jacob, into a patriarch of a nation, Israel.

The man is not Esau. The story, placing Jacob along a riverbank at dusk, plays off an ancient custom regarding the presence of river demons at nightfall. The author uses this unusual circumstance to his great advantage, for this "person" ends up blessing Jacob in a most unconventional manner: he changes his name. That takes place in verse 29. The mystery man refuses to provide his own name to Jacob and departs. The verses that follow (31–33) entail folk material about the name of the place. The passage includes the notion that Jacob thinks of his adversary as having been a deity, again echoing those traditions about night river demons.

In Judges 13 we also read of an encounter between an unsuspecting man and a divine being—albeit, one explicitly identified as such by the narrator. Only, the Judges passage is something of a parody, making fun of the dullard Manoah, who is to be the father of Samson. Manoah seeks to detain the angel with food, but the angel refuses because (naturally) angels do not consume food! The point is that Manoah fails to perceive the unusual nature of his guest, which results in his seeking to entertain him in ways that are irrelevant to divine entities. This is made explicit by the narrator:

> For Manoah did not know he was an angel of Yahweh. So Manoah said to the angel of Yahweh, "What is your name? We should like to honor you when your words [regarding the birth of a child] come true." The angel said to him, "What do you mean by asking for my name, for it is wondrous [pele']." (Judg 13:15–18)

Clearly this is the exact same scene as the one in Genesis 32. The response of the angel is word-for-word identical in both stories, although the stories differ with regard to other details. The Genesis story refers directly to the unnamed wrestler as *a man*, whereas the narrator in Judges informs the reader that this is an angel. And as noted, the goal in the Judges context is to make fun of Manoah, who does not even know an angel when one is staring him in the face. In contrast, Jacob is fighting with his aggressor at night, and we would not expect him to recognize him as other than a man. After all, Jacob holds his own in this physical struggle, something one would not expect to do with an angel. Combat with a mysterious adversary rather than the adversary Jacob and we, the readers, anticipate (namely, Esau) ends up being a struggle over peoplehood. One could not be sure which of Isaac's sons would become Israel, but with this story, it is clear that it will not be Esau, who is later designated father of the Edomites.

A single motif is used here for two very different stories. This provides us a rare window into the compositional methods of the Torah writers. While it is possible that one story borrowed the motif from the other, I would suggest it more likely that both writers drew from a common cultural paradigm. The core element is easily summarized: an unexpected encounter with a mysterious "person" results in a blessing of some sort. When that person's name is sought directly, he refuses disclosure and departs. The identity remains undetermined, but the blessing's content comes to fruition. Just how much of either story derives from some specific literary source rather than a more general cultural legend cannot be established. But what is so marvelously exposed is the artistry of both passages, which demonstrate how authors can mold a motif for different contexts and purposes. In one context, this motif is used to transform Jacob into Israel; in the other context, the motif is engaged to announce that a heretofore barren woman will give birth to the great Samson. Notice how a writer might have used the same motif to have Isaac's birth announced back in Genesis 18, but there a different narrative structure was engaged. And also notice that nothing intrinsic to the motif dictates how it might be used or adapted.

This is not the only time we have this particular window into the compositional methods of the Torah writers, but it is a particularly *wide* window.[1] It should be altogether clear that the authors worked from deep within their cultures, using imagery that, on the one hand, would be familiar to readers, and yet, on the other hand, could be employed creatively to yield meanings that a reader would not readily expect. In Oscar Wilde's dialogue "The Decay of Lying" (1891), the author, in the person of "Vivian," says, "Literature always anticipates life. It does not copy it, but moulds it to its purpose."[2] Our biblical authors understood this deeply. Their literature would, indeed, anticipate and shape Israelite identity through stories for millennia to come.

---

1. Numerous other examples are provided in my book *Etched in Stone*.

2. Oscar Wilde, "The Decay of Lying," in *The Complete Works of Oscar Wilde* (London: Hamlyn, 1963) 836.

10

Lost Literature

Introduction to the Joseph Story

The single longest narrative in the book of Genesis is the Joseph story (chapters 37–50, minus the interlude of chapter 38). The next four essays will treat general literary and ideological issues that are prominent in the Joseph story itself, while also bringing closure to the thematic concerns of Genesis. In this first essay on the Joseph story, I wish to explore the relevance of genre and lost literatures.

When we read literature today, we are at least subliminally aware of how various works intersect with other art forms, political events, and the like. My own kids, for instance, love reading fantasy and adventure novels. Though they might not articulate things with formal terminology, they readily recognize how aspects of any book they are reading have a lot in common with other books or films of the same genre. They can read Isabel Allende's legends of Zorro one week and see a *Star Wars* movie the next, understanding that Zorro's sword and Luke Skywalker's light saber are pretty much the same thing. When we read the Hebrew Bible, however, our ability to recognize what is drawn from a common, shared cultural repertoire is greatly hampered by certain insurmountable historical problems.

The form of our Hebrew Bible is the result of an editorial process known as canonization. As we discussed in chapter one, a canon is a closed set of works that some group, with sufficient authority, establishes as privileged and exclusive. The criteria for deeming a work worthy of inclusion within a canon can vary considerably. The most rigorous form of canon is that imposed by a religious community. When the authority figures of such a community establish a literary canon, the ideological values held by the ruling parties shape the selection process. Inevitably, the formation of a canon results in the demise of a great deal of literature. The Bible itself represents the quintessential religious canon, and there can be no doubt that many a book was lost because of its preeminence. The economics of literary production in antiquity required that someone have an interest in the copying of any given manuscript for reproductions to be commissioned. The dominant houses of scribes in antiquity were generally associated with monarchs and temples. Those institutions commissioned scribes to focus narrowly on works that furthered their interests, leaving the survival of other works to chance.

This may be difficult for moderns to fully grasp. We have such remarkable access to published works through library collections and the Internet that we take for granted the very notion of publication and dissemination. But if we imagine a book manuscript as akin to a letter we write by hand, we force ourselves to recognize what it might take to get the contents of that letter into the hands of a whole city, never mind an entire land. Even without the effects of canonization, it was inevitable that a great mass of literature would be lost over time. There is no way for us to even estimate just how much literature was actually lost in any given era, but what evidence does remain suggests that the quantity was sizable.

There are, for instance, fragments of old literature embedded in anthologies or quoted in contemporaneous writings that managed to survive. And then, periodically, there are those randomly discovered ancient manuscripts that shake our whole sense of the way the world was. Such discoveries were so numerous during the nineteenth and twentieth centuries that we could not possibly list them all here. But I wish to draw attention to one remarkable discovery, to illustrate just how complicated a matter it is to reconstruct a lost literary repertoire.

The most renowned discovery of manuscripts during the twentieth century is that of the Dead Sea Scrolls. The parchments found in a variety of caves near Qumran were copied predominantly during the last two centuries BCE. They appear to have been hidden in caves around the time that Jerusalem fell to the Romans in 70 CE. While the library sequestered at Qumran included every book of the Bible (except Esther), it also preserved writings of different political and religious parties whose identities have been lost. Some of these fragments are unique. Without them, we would know nothing of their contents' existence. Other documents found among the Dead Sea Scrolls managed to survive in isolated contexts for some time after the fall of the Second Temple.

An example of such a work emerged from the remarkable discovery of Jewish manuscripts made toward the end of the nineteenth century at the Ben Ezra Synagogue of Fustat, or "Old Cairo." There, Solomon Schechter uncovered the synagogue's geniza (the traditional storage place for damaged documents that bore Hebrew letters). The common practice among medieval Jewish communities was to stash damaged documents in a geniza until the community amassed enough material to be worthy of burial in a Jewish cemetery. For reasons unknown, the Fustat Jews allowed the contents of this unique stash to accumulate undisturbed from the late ninth century well into the nineteenth century. Among the manuscripts, Schechter identified and published a remarkable work he called *Fragments of a Zadokite Work*.[1] Nothing of this document was known before Schechter brought it to print. A bit more than three decades later, the Dead Sea yielded its famous Qumran scrolls. One container from Cave IV preserved parchments whose content agreed substantially with passages published by Schechter. In other words, the document hidden at Qumran around the turn of the first millennium remained in circulation long enough for some copyist to reproduced it for some (now unknown) patron during the tenth century CE. When it made its way into the Cairo Geniza is unknown. Without Qumran, we would never have been able to establish the antiquity of this document's origins. That is, we would simply have assumed its content derived from some era close to the time the manuscript was created. Had only the Qumran version but not the Cairo Geniza version survived, we would have believed the document disappeared with the hiding of the Qumran library. With the two together, separated by almost 1000 years, we are left with many more questions than answers. Who knew of this text after the documents at Qumran were hidden? What did they think of it? Why did it survive until the tenth century, but not beyond? Who owned it during the tenth century? Why did they commission its copying? What influence did its content have on those who read it? None of these questions are likely to be answered. But the fortuitous discovery of these two documents teaches a very important lesson: our knowledge of an ancient writer's cultural repertoire is very sparse. Before we make judgments regarding the meanings of stories, we need to remember the humble state of our cultural awareness when it comes to the world that produced our biblical stories. Without a

1 Solomon Schechter, *Fragments of a Zadokite Work*, Documents of Jewish Sectaries 1 (Cambridge: Cambridge University Press, 1910).

broad appreciation of the cultural repertoire from which the biblical writers drew their material, it is difficult to assess how writers stood against the backdrop of their own era. Were they innovators or conformists? Is their writing polemical or in harmony with dominant cultural trends? We can say very little about such important questions.

With these concerns in place, we turn to the story of Joseph (Genesis 37–50). Assuming one understands just what the clan of Jacob is, the Joseph story constitutes a freestanding novella. One could read this story from beginning to end and understand all of its scenes without having read anything that comes before it in the book of Genesis. What also emerges is that parts of the Joseph story were borrowed and adapted from literatures that were in circulation in antiquity. Consider, for instance, the scene responsible for landing Joseph in jail (Gen 39:5–21):

> [Potiphar] left all that he had in Joseph's hands and he didn't think about a thing except for the food he would eat. Joseph had become a well-built and handsome. Sometime later, his master's wife noticed Joseph and said, "Lie with me." But he refused, saying to his master's wife, "Look, with me here, my master doesn't give any thought to his household; everything he owns he has placed in my hands. He is not of a higher status in this house than I, and he has withheld nothing from me except yourself, given that you are his wife. How could I possibly do this terrible thing and also sin before God?" Even though she coaxed Joseph day after day, he did not yield to her request to be with her intimately. On a particular day, he entered the house to do his work. None of the household staff were present. She grabbed hold of him by his garment and said, "Lie with me!" But he left his garment in her hand and got away and fled outside. Seeing that he abandoned his garment with her while fleeing outside, she summoned her household servants and said to them, "Look, he brought us a Hebrew to dally with us! He approached me to lie with me; but I screamed loudly. When he heard me screaming at the top of my lungs, he abandoned his garment with me and got away outside." She held onto his garment beside her until his master returned home. Then she told him the same story: "The Hebrew slave whom you brought into our house came to me to dally with me; but when I screamed at the top of my lungs, he left his garment with me and fled outside." Upon hearing the story his wife told him, namely, "Thus and so your slave did to me," he was furious. So Joseph's master took and put him in prison, the very place where the king's prisoners were also confined. So he ended up there in prison.

This soap-opera-like scene derives from a literary motif that seems to have enjoyed considerable popularity in antiquity. While we cannot show direct dependence, Joseph's predicament with Potiphar's wife is not unlike that of Bata in the Egyptian legend known as "The Tale of Two Brothers." There we have two brothers, Anubis, the elder, and his kid brother, Bata, who lives with him and his wife. The two men are out working in the fields when they run out of supplies. Anubis sends his dutiful brother back to the village to retrieve additional sacks of seed. When Bata arrives, he finds his brother's wife braiding her hair. The young man takes hold of five heavy sacks of seed, a feat that proved quite impressive to his sister-in-law:

> Thereupon she said to him: "How much is what you have on your shoulder?" He said to her: "Three sacks of emmer and two sacks of barley, five in all, are on my shoulder," so he said to her. Then she [spoke to] him saying, "There is [great] strength in you. I see your vigor daily." And she desired to know him as a man. She got up, took hold of him, and said to him: "Come, let us spend an hour lying together. It will be good for you. And I will make fine clothes for you."

As is the case in the Mrs. Potiphar scene, the woman here is the instigator. And just like Joseph, righteous Bata will have nothing to do with this woman's advances. But, as is the case with Joseph, his innocence does him in:

> Then the youth became like a leopard in anger over the wicked speech she had made to him; and she became very frightened. He rebuked her, saying: "Look, you are like a mother to me; and your husband is like a father to me. He who is older than I has raised me. What is this great wrong you said to me? Do not say it to me again! But I will not tell it to anyone. I will not let it come from my mouth to any man." He picked up his load; he went off to the field . . .

Mrs. Potiphar (who lacks a personal name, just like Bata's sister-in-law) latches hold of some of Joseph's clothing and uses it as evidence against her husband's trusted servant. Bata's accuser is a bit more direct:

> When evening had come, his elder brother returned to his house . . . Now the wife of his elder brother was afraid on account of the speech she had made. So she took fat and grease and made herself appear as if she had been beaten, in order to tell her husband, "It was your brother who beat me."

Things don't go well for Bata from here on out. Were it not for a perspicacious talking cow, he would have stumbled into the living room, only to find his brother waiting with a dagger to kill him. There are enough differences between these tales to cast doubt on there having been a direct channel of influence. Nonetheless, the use of the same theme in the two stories—a female seducer who accuses her young male target of physical abuse after having her advances rebuffed—would suggest that the cultures that produced "The Tale of Two Brothers" and the scene in Potiphar's house drew from a common cultural repertoire.[2]

Unfortunately, we have very little access to the Hebrew literary repertoire of the biblical period beyond the Bible itself, and that makes it utterly impossible to tell just how many stories in Genesis (or the rest of the Bible) share elements with other freestanding Israelite compositions. As for non-Israelite literature, there is now a considerable body of scholarship demonstrating Israelite reliance on a great number of foreign sources for ideas, literary themes, and even expressions. But the ancient Near Eastern literature that has survived is also very limited in scope, leaving us to classify a great deal of our biblical narrative as unique. We will never know whether that uniqueness is, indeed, the result of Israelite ingenuity, or an accident of literary history—one that has denied us access to those influences that held sway over the literary artists of Hebrew Scriptures.

Reliance on either lost Israelite literature or foreign sources should not be seen as demoting the value of biblical literature. My goal here is simply to place the biblical narrative in its human perspective. The value of literature lies in the way it is *used,* not in its intrinsic characteristics. Fairy tales, which have no historical reality to them whatsoever, may still transmit many culturally rich messages. These messages are not compromised in our imagination's eye when common people, not unlike ourselves, are thrust into phantasmagoric scenarios, where the absurd and the mundane refuse to be distilled from one another. As we shall see in the next essay, the story of Joseph has a great deal to do with ancient Jewish fantasies about the shape of history itself. Despite the prevalence of many common social and literary tropes, there will be little commonplace about these imaginative renderings of the allegedly distant past, all of which are shaped for the sake of influencing the author's contemporary world.

2. The Egyptian passages are taken from the translations by Miriam Lichtheim, *Ancient Egyptian Literature*, 3 vols. (Berkeley: University of California Press, 1975) 2:203–5.

11

Absolute Exile

The most intractable theological conundrum of all monotheistic religions is the question of how God is manifest in history. Oftentimes the whole issue of divine involvement in historical events is distilled to the problem of evil and undeserved suffering—what is frequently labeled the problem of "theodicy." The issue can be framed simply as: if God is benevolent and able to act upon his sense of what is just, why do innocent people suffer? Almost as pressing is the problem of free will. If God has a hand in designing the unfolding of human affairs, how can free will be possible? Theologians since antiquity have contrived a vast array of thought games to get around the obviously irresolvable tensions that result when people insist on sustaining belief in a moral deity while also granting that deity power over the intricacies of nature and history alike. Attempts at rationalizing history in the presence of an ethical and potent deity generally result in three scenarios: (1) believers are required to suspend critical thinking and form a faith somehow unaffected by the travails of history they readily experience; (2) believers are required to accept and integrate the paradoxical into their approach to life; or (3) believers are required to withdraw into the mindset that our inability to resolve this tension is the result of our intellectual limitations and not something problematic about the ideas or, for that matter, God.

This essay is written for those who find all three scenarios unacceptable. If you are not such a reader, you will probably not find this essay terribly meaningful. But if, like me, you have grown thoroughly impatient with the "theological reasoning" that has no grounding in our daily experience of life, then perhaps this essay will prove satisfying. (Note: this is not an essay about whether God exists or not—that's quite a different discussion. The concern here is the history of belief regarding God, which is regularly grounded in biblical sources.)

I am starting from the position that the problem of theodicy—or God's responsibility for history in general—is a problem we should resolve by deconstructing its various components to expose its ill-formed foundations. The ideas that God engineers history, is incapable of evil, and is all-powerful have extremely shallow and fragmentary roots in biblical writings. The strong coalescence of these ideas, especially as they have been bantered about by Jewish and Christian theologians since antiquity, has its roots in that remarkable historical episode known as *Hellenization*—the collision of Hebrew narratives with Greek ("Hellenistic") philosophical ideas. These strange bedfellows—Hebrew and Hellene—whose relationship involved periods of insatiable attraction interspersed with deep mutual repulsion, spawned many offspring, one of which was *theology* itself. Until this fusion of cultures took place, no Jew thought "theologically." That is, no Jew thought to harmonize in a systematic way our experience of nature and history with some abstract, philosophically derived notion of God. It would never have occurred to a reader of Genesis to come up with a rationalization of history the way theologians do to this day. In most of the Hebrew Bible (not just Genesis), God functions as a character like many other characters. He has feelings, he changes his mind, he acts abruptly, he sometimes manifests deep concern and at other times shows insouciant indifference. Not a single verse in the book of Genesis attempts to justify or explain the character of God's powers over history or nature. Rather, it simply ascribes some acts to God and leaves others to the winds of personal discretion and chaos. There are, of course, among the verses of Psalms and the poesy of prophets, various claims as to God's powers over creation and the sustaining forces of nature. But no passage in our Hebrew Bible comes even remotely close to the kinds of contrived writing about Israel's patron deity as would be found *after* Judaism met Hellenism.

This, of course, does not mean that certain writers, among the panoply of authors whose works now make up Genesis, were not attuned to certain problems in the way history unfolded. This is especially true of the team of redactors who fashioned the final form of the book. I have advocated in these essays the principle that the core stories of Genesis existed in some literary form prior to their inclusion in the final document that now constitutes the first of five books in the Torah. Tensions among the various stories, which were not originally intended to be juxtaposed in the anthology before us, were inevitable. Making matters worse, the ideological overlay that holds the book together—those elements that elucidate the covenant regarding land, wealth, and progeny, as well as the genealogies— also caused narratives to chafe against one another and against the goals of the redactors themselves.

In the Joseph stories, that chafing resulted in a number of sores that the redactor could not let fester. If we step back to gaze upon the patriarchal narratives, from chapter 12 onward, we find ourselves in a series of short stories that are framed to facilitate the fulfillment of the ideological overlay. The patriarchs acquire wealth and eventually produce progeny—neither without divine intersession. The piece that is altogether missing is the land itself. The book of Genesis ends without acquisition of the "promised land." Theology aside, one readily notices that this problem with the narrative leaves the reader wondering why the redactor fashioned the story as he did. But before we address that concern, let us turn to a few passages that dramatically conflict with the overarching goals of the redactor.

The transference of Israelites from Canaan to Egypt is detailed in the following verses:

> The sons of Israel placed their father, Jacob, and their children
> and their wives in the wagons Pharaoh had sent to transport him.
> They also took their livestock and the moveable property they had
> amassed in the land of Canaan. Jacob with all his offspring came
> to Egypt: his sons and grandsons, his daughters and granddaugh-
> ters—all his offspring he brought to Egypt. (46:5–7)

These verses make clear that every living "Israelite" moved from Ca- naan—the Promised Land—to Egypt, a land that would initially host them hospitably, but eventually embitter their lives through forced enslavement. Obviously, the tension here emerges *only* if you know the book of Exo- dus. But imagine, for a moment, that the story in Exodus was unknown. Would Genesis have ended the same way? There is considerable evidence suggesting that the book once concluded differently. Imagine the Israelites living in Egypt just until the famine resolved itself. Based on Joseph's own predictions in Genesis 41, seven bad years would follow seven good years, meaning the famine would end fourteen years from the moment of Joseph's prediction. While in Egypt, as was the case with Jacob in Paddan-aram, the Israelites' numbers would increase, eventually allowing them to return to their promised land to experience the covenant fulfilled.

But this is not how our story turns out. Once the redactors of Torah decided to situate Genesis and Exodus as a progressive, chronologically linked set of narratives, Genesis could not possibly end with the Israelites back in Canaan. In other words, the original ending had to be dumped in order to accommodate a new and broader literary setting. The tensions between that original story and Exodus are not *real historical tensions*, they are *literary tensions*; intractable problems that emerge when you place, side-by-side, two narratives that were originally written independently of one another. Both, as it turns out, are historical allegories of eras long past, and they engage in a similar manner a number of common literary and thematic elements. Both stories involve Israel developing into a vast nation *in Egypt*. Both stories involve a lowly Israelite rising to powers derived from the Pharaoh's own household. Both use themes of slavery and liberation in a variety of ways.

Let us consider some of these elements in greater detail. Why would both Genesis and Exodus involve situating the ancient Israelites in Egypt? During the authors' own lifetime, the Diaspora of significance was in Mesopotamia. That is, after the destruction of the Temple in 586 BCE, there would develop a significant Jewish presence in what is today Iraq, Iran, Turkey, the Balkans, and beyond. The array of conquerors from Assyria, Babylon, Persia, and then Greece left Egypt a secondary power, at least when it came to dominating the Jewish homeland. Strategically speaking, it would be prudent to avoid writing a critical story about life in exile under the nose of the very conquerors whose subjects you had recently become. On the other hand, one could write safely about one's existential dilemma by allegorically referencing the present through imagery and events alleged to have taken place in a far-off land under rulers long dead. Once Persia fell to the Greeks—the first non-Mesopotamian power to factor into Middle Eastern politics in a "global" way—satires would arise regarding eastern lands as well, such as that of Esther, a Diaspora-based story which makes a travesty of the imaginary *eastern* kingdom of Shushan. The author of our Joseph story situated Israel's development in Egypt with the hope that Israel would return to the Promised Land as a great and mighty population. The story of Israel in Egypt put forth by the Exodus author was simply not part of the Genesis author's consciousness. (I'm differentiating the "author" of the stories from the "redactor" who organized them to produce what is now the book of Genesis, situated before Exodus.)

Conflicts between the stories, however, outnumber their commonalities. In the Joseph story we meet a most curious narrative about the development of Israel in Egypt. We are told that the famine was exceedingly severe, affecting the entire world (Genesis 47:13). Joseph's original plan was to store supplies during seven plentiful years so as to have supplies for the seven years of want. What was not elucidated in the initial plan was just how relentless Joseph would be in impoverishing the populace:

> There was no food anywhere in the land, for the famine had become severe; the lands of Egypt and Canaan languished because of the famine. Joseph collected together all of the monies remaining in the lands of Egypt and Canaan, as fees for the rations they procured. He brought the monies to Pharaoh's palace. When the money ran out in the lands of Egypt and Canaan, all the Egyptians came to Joseph, saying, "Provide us with food, lest we die right in front of you, because there's no money. Joseph said, "Bring your livestock, and I will leverage against your livestock, if the money is gone." So they brought their livestock to Joseph, and Joseph gave them food in exchange for the horses, flocks and cattle and asses; and he dispensed food for their livestock for that year. When that year was ended, they approached him for the second year saying to him: "We cannot hide from my lord that the money is spent and the flocks and livestock belong to my lord; nothing remains before my lord save for our bodies and lands. What good would it be if we died before your very eyes. Take us and our land as collateral for food and we and our land will be serfs for Pharaoh. He will provide seed so that we might live rather than die, and the land won't be ruined." This is how Joseph gained full possession of the farm land of Egypt for Pharaoh, for every Egyptian sold his field because the famine was just too much for them. The land became Pharaoh's. Subsequently, he transferred the population to cities, from one end of Egypt to the other. The priestly lands alone he did not acquire on a basis of an allotment Pharaoh himself had set for priests. They ate off the allotment which Pharaoh had stipulated for them; that's why they did not sell their land. Then Joseph said to the people, "Since, at this time, I have acquired your land for Pharaoh; here now is seed with which you should sow the land." When harvest-time arrives, you will give one-fifth to Pharaoh, and four-fifths will be yours as seed for the fields and for your food for in your households, and as nourishment for your children." And they said, "You saved our lives! Let us find favor in the eyes of our lord, and we will be Pharaoh's serfs." (47:13–25)

As the underlined phrases indicate, Joseph transformed the entire population of Egypt into what is commonly called corvée laborers. This was not an uncommon phenomenon in ancient Egypt. The Egyptian hierarchy regularly conscripted commoners into forced labor during those seasons of the year when agricultural workers—the vast majority of peasants—were idle. The evidence suggests that men, women, and children were all included in the corvée system.[1] A detail conveyed in the very last verse of Genesis 47 suggests that the Israelites were not only exempt from serving as slaves, but they somehow benefited from what amounts to insider trading: "Thus Israel settled in the country of Egypt, in the region of Goshen; they acquired holdings in it, and were fertile and increased greatly" (47:27).

Had the story ended there, Joseph, the man who reached Egypt as a slave sold to the house of Potiphar, would have engineered the acquisition of all Egyptian lands for his Pharaoh, the indenture of the starving countryside's populace when they were most vulnerable, and the enrichment of his own family—Jacob's descendants. Thus, the Joseph story would have resolved two parts of the covenant's details—wealth and progeny. All that was left was a return to the land.

That the enrichment and proliferation are the result of a divine hand in history is also blatant. One might have thought Joseph would bear something of a grudge against his cruel brothers. But our story's author dispenses with that concern quite readily in three verses:

> Now, don't become depressed or angry regarding yourself because you sold me here; God sent me here before you to save lives. There's been famine in the land for two years; there's another five years to go, during which there will be neither tilling nor harvesting. God sent me ahead of you to ensure for you a remnant on earth, and to save your lives in a great survivorship. So actually, it was not you who sent me here, but God; He situated me as a father to Pharaoh, and as lord over his household, and ruler over the entire land of Egypt. (45:5–8)

With yet deeper ironic overtones, the same sentiment is conveyed a few lines from the very end of the book. Once Jacob has died, the brothers worry that Joseph might exact revenge. "We are prepared to become your slaves," they proclaim. The brothers who despised Joseph's early interpretation of dreams, all of which entailed subordination to him, now happily

---

1. For a brief overview, see Kathryn A. Bard, ed., *Encyclopedia of the Archaeology of Ancient Egypt* (London: Routledge, 1999) 745.

accept the role. But for those of us aware that barely a paragraph separates us from beginning the book of Exodus, we are not sure whether this is ironic foreshadowing or a coincidence of imageries that was fostered by the fusing of these two works into one volume.

These passages should not be confused with a post-Hellenistic, theologically charged concept of divine determinism. Notice, God manages to engineer *some* aspects of history, but not others. After all, were he all-powerful and ethically good in the conventional theological sense, it would be reasonable to wonder why he would tolerate a famine in the first place—a natural disaster that affects the wicked and the kind, the adult and the child indiscriminately. But such questions did not occur to the writer of this story and they should not play a role in our own reading strategy. Authors cannot address questions that never occur to them. The Genesis author had no problem whatsoever with a God who had a *limited influence over history*. Indeed, he never imagined attributing all events to divine fiat. If this issue strikes us, as modern readers, as a problem in the narrative, then we have (perhaps unwittingly) acquiesced to the postbiblical theologian's preference for language games. Such theologians continue to foist upon contemporary readers the notion that everything in history must fit into a nice neat package, because God does not involve himself in contradictions. But the reality of God is a local-literary, rather than a global-literary, phenomenon. Each author depicts history and God the way he or she thinks best, and not according to the way (theologians think) the world works. Different approaches result in altogether irresolvable tensions, not because the real world naturally harbors paradoxes but because humans harbor dissonant perspectives on life and history. Voices clash when we insist on hearing them all at once. Attuned to their distinctiveness, we might facilitate hearing discrete melodies more clearly. And in the end, perhaps we will choose to sing along with one rather than another.

12

Fantasy, Ancient Jewish Style

Surely the most fanciful aspect of the entire Joseph story is the status achieved by Joseph in the administration of the Egyptian monarchy. Upon interpreting a dream regarding matters of "national security," Pharaoh ascribes to Joseph the "spirit of God" and straightaway places him in charge of his people's administration. "According to your command," Pharaoh tells him, "all my people will be directed; only regarding the throne will I remain superior to you" (41:40).

If we relate to this literature as history, we will apply the wrong genre criteria in evaluating its meaning. There is no evidence of there ever having been an Israelite who governed over Egypt. Attempts to link Joseph with historical personages or to sketchy references in ancient annals to short-lived foreign rulers all fail. This is not history. We have here a Cinderella-like fairy tale, where the despised brother not only ends up making good but, of all things, ascends to the most powerful political position in a foreign land, barely a notch below the authority of the monarch himself. Moreover, what gets him there is the interpretation of dreams, a symbolic activity meant to represent a form of divinely sanctioned wisdom—but here, wisdom put to work in exile and quite distinct from other forms of sign-reading that are associated with priests, prophets, and temples.

I think it fair to say that kings do not regularly promote men who are prisoners on Monday to chief of staff on Tuesday. In real life, we should imagine that a king's loyal advisors would be less than pleased about being bypassed for this prized position, not to mention subordinated to a former Hebrew slave of unknown origins. One is expected to suspend all calls for plausibility in fairy tales because the rules of this literary genre demand as much. Were we to seek historical feasibility, we would be ignoring all of those literary signals that instruct us on how to read and understand this story. This is fantasy, pure and simple, but fantasy with deep meanings.

The book of Genesis is ostensibly about the creation of a clan that has a privileged status *vis-à-vis* a patron deity. That status is to be expressed through three rewards: possession of a land, the production of progeny, and the accumulation of wealth. Strangely enough, Genesis never raises the question of governance, either in terms of a monarchy or a priestly oligarchy. How odd that a people, in writing of its origins, fails to mention the ascendancy of its king, or even outline the structure of its governing bodies. Of course, later in Israel's history there will be chronicles of various kings and stories of clan leaders, but these are written subsequent to or independent of the book of Genesis. The books of Samuel, Kings, and Chronicles are later attempts at more normative annals, bringing Israelite narratives somewhat more in line (thematically and structurally) with those of foreign peoples.

But I am speaking here of the Jews' origination stories, not depictions of later historiographic eras. The evidence suggests that in all other cultures of the ancient world, the kings themselves were quite keen on having told the very stories that linked their own family's ascendancy to the crown. But this is not the case in Genesis. Strangely enough, Exodus will also avoid this theme. Indeed, *the entire Torah* ignores the question of indigenous governance beyond that of the priestly caste (Levites) and clan patriarchs, save for one brief passage in Deuteronomy, which reads as follows:

> If, upon entering the land that the LORD your God has provided you, and upon taking full possession of it and settling in it, you decide, "I will appoint a king over me, as do all the surrounding nations," you will be free to appoint over yourself a king, whom the LORD your God will choose. You will appoint as king over you only someone from among your kinsmen. You are not to appoint a foreigner over you, one who is not your kinsman. (Deut 17:14–15)

Notice that God does not actively promote the establishment of a monarchy; according to this brief passage, it is simply left as a matter of choice. In other ancient Near Eastern cultures, where covenants between gods and kings are the foundations for the patron-vassal structure on which nations are built, legends tell of a monarch's illustrious rise to power made possible through divine favors. The contrast with Israelite literature is simply overwhelming. The Torah neither requires nor even predicts the establishment of a monarchy. What could account for such an approach? I would suggest that had there been a king in Israel when this literature was composed, Deuteronomy 17 would not have left monarchy a mere *option*. No king would lend support to an official history that does not include his ascendancy as divinely ordained (or at least historically inevitable). But none of the Torah books predict or call for a king. Rather, they offer remarkable alternatives to the role of king.

There is, of course, Moses. He is a man raised and educated among (Egyptian) royalty, but upon assuming the leadership of his own people, he is called prophet rather than king. Moreover, he produces no heir as kings are wont to do. His successor, Joshua, is a military man turned prophet, bearing no familial relationship to his mentor. And true to form, Joshua himself leaves no heir. This unconventional paradigm is an Israelite creation, with no literary or historical antecedent known to us.

Indeed, it is an act of ingenuity to frame leadership as possible outside of the monarchic model. But it is not this model of leadership alone that proves at odds with historical precedent; it is the *place* of that leadership. Moses will reign over Israel *in Egypt and in a vast wilderness*, not in a Jewish land. The greatest Jewish leader of all times reigns *in the Diaspora*.

Similarly, there is deep irony in the fact that Joseph becomes an *almost-king* in Egypt, but like Moses, leaves no heirs eligible to serve as Israel's future redeemer. He is quite specifically framed as the redeemer for his present generation, but with the themes that will become "traditional" for redeemers turned on their heads. Upon disclosing his identity to his brothers, Joseph proclaims:

> God sent me ahead of you to ensure for you a remnant on earth, and to save your lives in a great survivorship. So actually, it was not you who sent me here, but God; He situated me as a father to Pharaoh, and as lord over his household, and ruler over the entire land of Egypt. (Gen 45:7–8)

The vocabulary alone should strike us as discordant. The redeemer is made "ruler" of *a foreign land*; "survivorship" (ostensibly from the famine in Canaan) occurs through peaceful transference into an exilic sojourn. How bizarre that this origination story should focus on survival as requiring displacement from the Promised Land through a leader whose rise from slave to lord over a foreign land—their place of redemption—is choreographed by God.

The particulars of Genesis are rendered irrelevant by a verse at the opening of Exodus, which tells us a new king arose who knew nothing of Joseph's era (1:8). This is one more method of distancing Jewish history from the normal patterns assumed by other peoples. Israel's first redeemer transfers the people from Canaan to Egypt; but Israel's second redeemer is destined to reverse the path. Only, that second redeemer will come *not* from the house of the man who, for all intents and purposes, ruled as king in Egypt—Joseph. Instead, the second redeemer will hail from the House of Levi, the very clan that will never hold land in Israel and whose power will emerge through priestly rather than monarchic authority. At each and every point of the storyline, conventional thinking about leadership, inheritance, and monarchy are undermined.

Joseph speaks Egyptian and marries Egyptian women; Moses is raised as an Egyptian and marries a Midianite and a Cushite. Somehow, the history of interpretation has downplayed these profound depictions of Jewish life in exile, where positions of power imply a kind of social integration that is figuratively represented by the taking of foreign wives.[1] The conflicted attitudes toward life in the Diaspora, which pit clan-allegiance against the desire for power and stability, perhaps dwell just beneath the surface of the secondary phrase in the Deuteronomic passage noted above: "Be sure to set as king over yourself one of your own people; you must not set a foreigner over you, one who is not your kinsman." The entire book of Deuteronomy retells events that took place prior to the Israelites' completion of their forty years of wandering in the wilderness. Consequently, if you read this as pertaining to a sojourn in the land of Israel, it must be concerned with a "future era," when the danger of governance falling to a conquering power would make sense. And such a reading is surely plausible. But more valid, in my opinion, is to understand this as a comment about Jews living in foreign lands. In their own land, while enjoying independence and sovereignty, a people would hardly think to entertain a foreign leader, unless it is forced upon them—a scenario Deuteronomy does not allude to in any context. But if you are living in a foreign land, the question of allegiance becomes particularly thorny. By making Joseph an *almost-king* in Egypt, the Jews could think of themselves as having lived under the aegis of someone from amongst themselves. And the same would be true when Moses emerges

1. Keep in mind Solomon's excesses along these lines, including 700 wives taken from among the Moabites, Ammonites, Edomites, Zidonites, Hittites, and, of course, the Egyptians (1 Kings 11:1–3); but all that takes place on Israelite rather than foreign soil and is readily condemned by the authors.

as ruler of Israel in Egypt and the wilderness. In effect, when in exile, it is hoped that Jews will not sacrifice control over their own cultural destiny, as they might otherwise be expected to do. The hope was that Jews, through merit, would ultimately rise to positions of power even in foreign lands (like Joseph), thereby guaranteeing cultural autonomy. Such a structure would enable them to think of themselves as having a "kinsman" ruling over them.

Alas, it is all fantasy—there was never an Israelite in Egypt who reigned from the house of Pharaoh, nor was there in the ancient world a Jew who rose to rule a foreign land quite like Joseph. But it is a fantasy born of anguished times, when the pressures to assimilate into an inhospitable world of competing cultures forced Jews to imagine new approaches to survival. Till that time, the world had not imagined it possible for a people to preserve a cultural identity without enjoying the stability of traditional sovereigns in a land all their own. Through a parable about survival in exile, we are to learn that history can be defied.

13

Ideological History

The concluding sections of Genesis have two roles: they provide closure through a burial theme and they create a bridge to the Exodus story. At the end of Genesis 49 Joseph swears to his father, Jacob, that he will deliver his body to their ancestral burial place, the cave of Machpelah, at the field near Mamre, first acquired by Abraham (see our discussion in chapter 6). In this sense, the Joseph story, while serving as a bridge to Exodus by explaining why Israel moved to Egypt in the first place, also allows for Jacob's burial to take place on what was considered ancestral ground. But this close tie to the land of the forbearers is only half of the quotient at play in this scene. Genesis tells us that Jacob lived 147 years (47:28). More than twenty of those years were spent in Padan-aram (Mesopotamia) and the final seventy years of his life passed in Egypt. In effect, Jacob was a Jew of the Diaspora. While his entire retinue accompanies his bones back to Machpelah (50:8), not one person from the burial party remains there. Indeed, not a single Israelite from the generations of the patriarchs is portrayed as settling and remaining in the Promised Land. Half a millennium later, Joshua will arrive very much the way Abraham arrived—as a newcomer.

Echoing this focus on burial in the Promised Land, Joseph "made the sons of Israel swear" that they, too, would transfer his bones "homeward." The Torah's editors would use this oath as a vehicle for linking together the various parts of the story that extends from Genesis to Joshua. In Exodus 13:19 we learn that "Moses took with him the bones of Joseph," and in Joshua 24:32, when the people finally settles in their designated home and, those bones are laid to rest in Shechem.[1]

1. The passage reads, "The bones of Joseph, which the Israelites had brought up from

When Genesis concludes, one part of the original covenant remains unfulfilled—land acquisition. I have noted at various points in these essays that the composition of the individual stories and the anthologizing process that produced Genesis occurred prior to the formation of the Torah's big picture. That is, the discrete stories emerged from a literary context that was unrelated to the program that ultimately motivated the redactor. The freestanding origins of our Genesis stories sometimes result in thematic dissonances within the narrative. The failure of the Genesis story to conclude with the fulfillment of all three aspects of the covenant is an example of such a thematic dissonance. But that very absence speaks to the Diaspora theme that flows through the Genesis narrative.

Covenants are imagined; people's lives unfold as they will. The authors of the Genesis narrative sustained their allegorical representation of Jewish diaspora living through to this very Genesis chapter. They hoped people would identify with the generations of old—generations that overcame the challenges of "exile," ultimately to reassemble in the ancient lands. The reader was supposed to see him- or herself as living a life not unlike the patriarchs and matriarchs themselves, a reading strategy that becomes explicit in Deuteronomy with the notion that even future generations are, in some sense, *present* throughout the wilderness experience (see Deuteronomy 29).

Sensitivity to the plight of the diaspora dweller emerges throughout Genesis. Even with the tender depiction of Jacob's burial, we are reminded of the Jew's tenuous exilic existence. Mourning for Jacob takes place not in the homeland, but at *Goren ha-Atad*, "which is beyond the Jordan" (50:11)—that is, in the diaspora. Burial in one's ancestral lands would remain an ideal for Jews throughout the centuries. The bitter historical reality, however, was that most Jews would die "in exile" and most mourning—like that for Jacob by the entirety of the Israelite nation—would take place wherever the passing of a loved one occurred. Thus, the force of the narrative is to reflect upon the *lives* of the patriarchal and matriarchal generations, lives which unfolded predominantly in exile—their idealized burials notwithstanding. Prior to the founding of the modern state of Israel, their lives reflected the realities of most Jews throughout history.

Egypt, were buried at Shechem, in the piece of ground which Jacob had bought for a hundred *kesitahs* from the children of Hamor, Shechem's father, and which had become a heritage of the Josephites." The acquisition referred to is noted in Genesis 33:19, but why this was designated Joseph's burial place is uncertain.

14

Entering Exodus

Why end a book called *Genesis Ideology* with a chapter called *Entering Exodus*? The five books that comprise the Torah tell stories of Israel's origins in two discrete developmental stages. The first book, Genesis, fosters ethnic identity by suggesting that all Israelites derive from Jacob and four women, Leah, Bilhah, Rachel, and Zilpah. As such, the primary emphasis of Genesis is the creation of a people through *endagomy*, that is, marriage among a distinct cluster of clans, all of which descend from Jacob, the son of Isaac, the son of Abraham. As for what distinguishes Israelite culture or religious practices from those of other Canaanite peoples, the book of Genesis provides very few details. We learn that Abraham and his descendants were in a unique relationship with their God called יהוה (commonly rendered *Yahweh*, Gen 15:7), but the book is nearly silent regarding rituals, beliefs, and social customs that might have distinguished the Israelites from their neighbors. The authors of Genesis were concerned with creating a feeling of unity based on the concept of blood relations; group identity formed on the basis of life practices was not part of their literary agenda.

In contrast, the Torah's subsequent books, starting with Exodus, entail narratives that focus on the *content* of Israelite life and socio-political organization. Genesis ends with the Israelites forced to sojourn in Egypt to escape a famine. While they are successful at integrating into Egyptian society during the lifetime of Joseph, son of Jacob, the story suggests a degradation of living circumstances upon Joseph's demise. It is then that the general population is enslaved so as to undermine their ability to pose a military threat to the Egyptian monarchy. Outside of the Hebrew Bible, there are no literary or archaeological voices corroborating the historicity of an Israelite enslavement lasting some 430 years (as suggested by Exod 12:40); nor are there sources verifying a mass exodus of people as numerous as the Israelites allegedly were at the time of their redemption (see Exod 12:37, purporting an exodus of 600,000 men alone). This should not come as a surprise. Just like the narratives in Genesis, the story of Israel in Egypt was originally fashioned as allegory representing the historical experience of exile experienced by the writers' own generation. The story of Israel in Egypt reflects the authors' strategies for generating cultural and religious identity, as well as hope, so that their generation might be able to cope with an increasingly dispersed peoplehood. In its final state, the story crafted by Israelite scribes during the post-exilic period (after 535 BCE) constitutes a virtuosic achievement designed to do all that Genesis leaves incomplete: the creation of a literature that would generate cultural content and identity even in the face of a seemingly hopeless state of defeat at the hands of Babylonian armies. In a sense, to grasp what Genesis sought to accomplish and left unfinished, one needs to understand what the Exodus story seeks to bring about.

Israel in Egypt is the story of an oppressed people living far removed from a homeland, without the organizational structures enjoyed by all other autonomous ancient civilizations: a monarchy, a priestly caste with permanent cultic sites, and most important, a land of their own. How, then, might the people survive such circumstances? Exodus's authors would fuse together older literary traditions and images of the land of Pharaohs with newly invented cultural solutions. Genesis had already stipulated that Abraham and his descendants could relate directly to their God without an intermediary, both in the land of Israel and in Mesopotamia (Padan-Aram). The Exodus authors continue that theological premise, while building upon the God–people relationship by integrating commitments to law, custom, and ritual.

When reading Genesis, one recognizes that history was altered through the meeting of Yahweh and Israel's ancestors—Abraham, Isaac, and Jacob. By reading Exodus, one comes to understand that God spoke to Moses first in the wilderness, shaped history, and delivered the Tablets of the Decalogue not from Jerusalem's Mount Zion (compare Isa 2:3), but in the midst of an uncharted desert belonging to no single tribe or clan. Abraham evokes the creation of Israel; Moses brings about its redemption from exile. Israel's great redeeming leader was not a king but a man who merged the wisdom of a sage-teacher with the insights of a prophet bearing

God's will. The underlying message of the entire narrative is at once simple and idealistic: if the Israelite people could survive the horrors of servitude under the whips of Pharaoh's taskmasters, they can survive their present challenges of dispersion in Babylon and other lands. The story suggests that redemption by God was possible even in that most extreme of situations. No matter where the Jew is situated, God's voice can be heard and his hand in history felt. The allegory may have been situated in a remote time and place, but for the post-exilic world, its lessons were the source of hope and perseverance, both within the homeland and in far-off lands.

Today's readers of Torah are often so acclimated to the biblical narrative that they might not recognize just how creative the Exodus narrative was in its own day, or how radical. Over the centuries, the allegory was literalized into "history," doing a terrible disservice to the inventiveness of the book's authors. Exile was real, of course, but the allegory permitted the authors to displace blame from the perpetrators who still held sway over Israel's destiny when they shifted it to a then-weakened Egyptian kingdom. The creation of Moses as a king-like prophet constitutes one of the more ingenious inventions of the Exodus writers. Outside of the Torah, many so-called early prophetic writings, such as those of Amos and Hosea, convey awareness of God's redemption of Israel from Egypt, but no pre-exilic Hebrew literature makes mention of Moses, Aaron, and Miriam.[1] The climactic scene of Moses's career, the giving of the Ten Commandments on stone tablets on Mount Sinai, is mentioned in no other biblical passage outside of the Torah, save for a single verse in 1 Kings (8:9)—a late, ideologically charged interpolation intent on dispelling the notion that God actually "lives" in the ark.

The present form of Exodus is the result of multiple stages of development. We recognize this by virtue of a number of story fragments that were obviously reshaped within the narrative by subsequent editors. For instance, in Exodus 4, when Moses asks God for a way to convince the Israelites that his authority derives from their ancestral deity, God provides Moses a series of magic tricks. As the story unfolds, these magic tricks fail to appear in the scene introducing Moses to the Israelite slaves, but are instead revamped and integrated into Moses's first appearance before

1. Micah 6:4 reads, "I sent before you Moses, Aaron, and Miriam," but the date of this text cannot be determined. It is the only mention of the three siblings together outside of the Pentateuch. Jeremiah (15:1) pairs Moses with Samuel when speaking of Israel's heroic intercessors on behalf of the people before God. Moses appears in no other pre-exilic prophetic writing.

Pharaoh and his courtiers (ch. 7). The failure of these tricks to impress Pharaoh provides the authors with the opportunity to integrate an extended story of divinely sanctioned plagues. In Exodus the plagues are ten in number (chs. 7–12), but in Psalms 78 and 105, only seven are mentioned (with slightly different terminology for some plagues), likely representing an earlier stage of the story's development. Additionally, there are reasons to see the plagues as emerging somewhat in conflict with what might have been the originally planned redemption scene involving God's splitting of the Sea of Reeds before the charging Egyptian army (ch. 15). The present story has two climactic scenes: that of the tenth plague, which results in the invention of the Passover ritual, and that of the defeat of Pharaoh's army at the Sea of Reeds (or "Red Sea"). Both, however, accomplish the same thing: they demonstrate the power of Israel's God over the forces of history, both natural and human.

The plague narrative provocatively yielded the invention of the *pesach* ritual. The authors integrated what appears to have been an ancient practice of painting doorposts with blood to fend off evil spirits with the final plague, "death of the firstborn." The generic custom was re-mythologized, transforming what appears to have been a common apotropaic (protection) ritual into the specific act performed by Israelites on that very night to prevent the "Destroyer" (המשחית) from entering their households. Although the common rendering of the word *pesach* is "Passover," in chapter 12 of Exodus the term unequivocally means "to protect." This is made explicit when we read: "For the LORD will pass through (עבר) to smite the Egyptians, but he will see the blood on the lintels and doorposts and *protect* (ופסח) the entrances, not permitting the Destroyer to enter into their [the Israelite] homes to smite [them]" (Exod 12:23).

The use of *matzah* as an aspect of the redemption scene is less elegantly integrated. Unleavened breads were a standard component of the sacrificial cult (see Lev 4:2, 13, 22, et al.). It is most likely the case that a celebration of springtime crops entailed special foods, some associated with the eating of slaughtered animals and others, perhaps, associated with the harvest itself. When *matzah* is first introduced in Exodus 12, there is no intrinsic relationship between the *pesach* slaughter and the unleavened bread (12:15–20). The writer of the book of Deuteronomy, who removed the practice of slaughtering an animal at the observer's home and made it an exclusively temple-oriented "sacrifice" (cf. Deut 16), emphasized *matzah* as the principal non-cultic observance of common Jews at their homes. The last part of Exodus 12 was eventually harmonized with Deuteronomy's notion that non-leavening flatbreads were consumed because there was insufficient time for the bread to rise on the night that the Egyptians cast Israel out of their land (see Deut 16:3). The notion that the breads could not rise (Exod 12:39) is in direct conflict with the overall demeanor of the chapter's first verses, which suggests that the animal used to protect Israelite homes was designated a full four days before the slaughter would take place, leaving plenty of time to prepare the meal adequately. Moreover, according to the *pesach* aspect of the story, there could not have been a nighttime departure (as is suggested in Exod 12:31) given that the success of the ritual is predicated on the notion that the Israelites would remain within their homes until daybreak so as to take advantage of the bloodstained doorposts inviting divine protection. As modern readers, we should embrace these tensions within the story's evolution as suggestive of how diverse schools of thought struggled to shape Jewish practices. In effect, we end up with multiple "Exodus Ideologies." Today, Jews celebrate Passover with *matzah,* while the protective home slaughter ritual is only symbolically preserved by placing a lamb's shank bone on the Seder Plate.

Unlike Genesis, which shows the imprint of fewer ideological accommodations, Exodus likely underwent a few stages of development. At its core is the story of Israel in Egypt (chs. 1–14), which concludes with their crossing the Sea of Reeds (ch. 15). With the second part of chapter 15 (vv. 22–27) there commences a series of scenes that portray Israel's Wilderness Sojourn as fraught with stresses over leadership and survival. The Wilderness Sojourn becomes a repository for situating a variety of literary genres, each of which permits its authors to address questions of practice, belief, leadership structures, and identity. Many of these stories (in Exodus and Numbers) reinforce the authority of Aaron and his descendants as High Priests. Entire sections of Exodus (chs. 25–31 and 35–40) address issues only concerning the priesthood's cultic responsibilities.

The scene at Mount Sinai (chs. 19–20) was not likely part of the book's original design, but it would spawn some of the most significant religious symbols in the history of Judaism. In God's presence, Moses fashions a legal system with two types of documents. The first entails the fashioning of two stone tablets, symbolic of God's covenantal relationship with Israel as being founded upon a basic ethical code. The second part includes more extensive legal judgments, frequently referred to as "The Covenant Code" (Exod 21–24). Here again, we see imaginative innovation at work. The standard symbol of a covenantal agreement among many ancient Near Eastern cultures was the standing stone (מצבה). When Jacob is portrayed as establishing a border agreement between his clan and that of Laban, both men erect the equivalent of standing stones (Gen 31:46). Similar objects appear prominently in Joshua 4 (vv. 3, 8, 9) and 8:29. Such monuments were supposed to evoke awareness of covenantal relations between various parties, or alternatively, a people and their God. For a Diaspora community, the disadvantage of this symbol is that it is fixed in the ground where the covenant was first established and not where the people might be located. A symbolic stone erected at Mount Sinai, located far from Israel's desired homeland, could hardly have served its purpose of evoking remembrance of a heroic past. To accommodate the evocative nature of this symbol, the Exodus author invents the *portable stone tablet*, eventually to be housed and carried through the wilderness in the Ark of the Covenant. So as not to completely bypass the original symbol, Moses is also said to have erected 12 stones, one for each of Israel's tribes, at the end of his 40 days on Mount Sinai (Exod 24:4). But these are distinct from the tablets that contain God's actual writing. The portable tablets reinforce the notion that God can establish a covenant of law with the Jews anywhere without foregoing the power implicit in the symbol of standing stones.

The content of the Decalogue is decidedly secular, save for one ethnically based religious commandment—observance of the Sabbath. The school responsible for the contents of the Decalogue was apparently sensitive to how Israelites might appear to other peoples, both within the region of Israel's homeland and in the Diaspora. Thus, the Ten Commandments commence by stipulating Israel's unique relationship with a principal deity, which would have emulated how other peoples in the region expressed allegiance to their own local deities. The core of the commandments, however, is totally in harmony with what every other culture in the region valued: prohibitions against theft, murder, adultery, and behaviors thought to threaten sovereignty over property. The design of these commandments and the "Covenant Code" that follows, were meant to suggest that the Israelites had achieved a level of civilization at least equal to those associated with the law-giving monarchies dating back to the recesses of antiquity, with the most celebrated being King Ur-nammu (Sumer, twenty-first century BCE), Lipit-Ishtar (nineteenth century BCE), and the monarchy of Hammurabi (eighteenth century BCE). The writers of Deuteronomy make this concern for achieving parity among the nations of the world explicit when they write that the laws will serve as "proof of [Israel's] wisdom and discernment to other peoples, who, upon hearing these laws will think, 'Surely this great people is a wise and thoughtful people'" (Deut 4:6).

Not every ideological school was enamored with the secular Decalogue that would find its way to Exodus 20. A counter narrative was composed by priestly intellectuals who portrayed God's covenantal document quite differently. The story of the "Golden Calf" (Exodus 32–34) depicts Moses destroying the initial tablets—symbolically representative of the "secular" Decalogue—when he witnesses the idolatrous (assimilationist) observances of the people who fashioned a surrogate for Moses's leadership during his forty-day absence on Mount Sinai. Going back up the mountain, Moses would ultimately deliver the version of the covenant that we read in Exodus 34. It is highly ethnocentric in character, commencing with a prohibition against assimilation amidst adjoining populations, which includes a stern condemnation of intermarriage and the production of idols (34:12–17). The edicts then continue with observance of the Matzah Festival (v. 18), dedication of the first born to God (vv. 19–20), the observance of Sabbath (v. 21), Feast of Weeks (*Shavuot*, v. 22) and the other festivals as pilgrimage observances, etc. It is beyond the scope of this essay to discuss why both versions of the Decalogue were preserved by the final editors of Exodus; what is clear, however, is that the book's editors regularly preserved various (even divergent) perspectives on Israel's formation, taking advantage of the core indeterminacy of all allegorical stories.

Based on practices already evident within the Torah, the Exodus would become the paradigm for all discourse concerned with future redemption. Additionally, rituals that ostensibly had little to do with the original Exodus "event" would be integrated into the dominant themes of the Exodus—particularly, God's intercession as a historical force. As such, just as the *pesach* slaughter itself was likely a generic apotropaic rite, the other pilgrimages ultimately associated with the Exodus appear to have had their origins in agricultural practices, or in the case of *Sukkot*, an ancient Enthronement Ritual, cognizance of which is still preserved in the Mishnah Rosh Hashanah (1:1 "the first of Nisan is a new year for kingship and pilgrimages"). Similarly, the use of *totafot*, or "amulets," on straps affixed to the forehead and arm, was depicted as a normative heuristic device by the Deuteronomist for teaching future generations about God's law-based covenant (Deut 6:8; 11:18). The dominant imagery in those contexts is not the Exodus from Egypt, but the origins of the covenant with Abraham, Isaac, and Jacob (Deut 6:10 and 11:21–25). In contrast, Exodus 13:16 associates the use of *totafot* with the Exodus story, noting that they are placed on the hand and forehead to evoke cognizance of God's deliverance from Egypt by "a mighty hand." The Ashkenazic morning ritual of *tefillin* alludes to this verse ("Let us remember the miracles and wonders that [God] did for us when he took us out of Egypt"). Remembrance of the Exodus from Egypt is a central component of principal liturgical components in the daily worship ritual, including the recitation of Exodus 15 prior to the morning "Call to Worship." In Exodus 20:11 Sabbath observance is justified as emulating God's desire for rest on the seventh day. This justification was not attractive to the Deuteronomist thinkers, who objected to anthropomorphic depictions of Israel's God. Thus, in Deuteronomy 5:15, Sabbath observance is justified as a remembrance of what it was like to have been slaves, working without rest. The later rabbinic sanctification of the Sabbath with wine draws upon both themes.

It is fair to say that the dominance of the literary imagery of Exodus remained constant through the Second Temple Period and into the Rabbinic Era, especially with the fashioning of Passover rituals in the *Haggadah shel Pesach*. Each Jew was to imagine having participated in the redemption experience of the ancient Israelite, fostering a constant empathy for those whose lives were oppressed and inspiring hope in all Jews who would imagine a return to the Promised Land.

Epilogue

There is no feasible way to establish with certainty the relative significance of any given cause in history without being able to replay the events with different variables in place. History permits no such experimentation. Theories of dynamical systems—of which history is certainly one—often bring to bear the notion of "sensitive dependency on initial conditions." This is commonly called the "butterfly effect," a term coined by the MIT professor Edward Lorenz. The idea is that even the most seemingly innocuous flapping of a butterfly's wings can have implications for the unfolding of events around the globe. This means that we cannot know what consequences will derive from which conditions, because the sheer number of variables at play—most of which remain invisible to us—is simply too great. We are left to ascribe causality to those things we can see and we do not even entertain those causes that are outside our immediate field of vision. Even among those factors we can perceive, our ability to understand which ones serve as pivotal, among the infinite array of historical forces, is minimal. In a given scenario, Factor A may appear meaningless; a slight shift in focus renders Factor A a determinative force.

Today, approximately 2,500 years removed from the authors who framed Genesis and Exodus, we might wonder what the history of Judaism and the world would have been like if these books had never been written, or had been written differently, or had not succeeded in achieving canonical status. Some might say such speculation is a banal exercise. The reality of Genesis and Exodus, they might argue, and its history of interpretation are historical facts not to be toyed with on the basis of some hypothetically reengineered history.

And yet, the writing of one book and its survival is precisely an accident of history for which we are unable to establish cogent causes. Genesis offered its target generation an idea of how to think of itself; the Exodus writers, seeing a lack, offered a book about how to conduct oneself. Both books unfold predominantly in a state of exile. Both tell the story of a minor ethnos among the peoples of the ancient world, using literary themes quite unlike anything found among the Near Eastern cultures of the time. Of those other cultures, all that remains are fragments of their literary work for scholars to examine and material artifacts for archaeologists to excavate. Not a single work from ancient Mesopotamia, Egypt, or Canaan developed a history of interpretation that would spawn an ongoing cultural engagement. I believe this fact demands reflection, if for no other reason than to consider the potential for emulating today the forces at work behind the promulgation of literature.

Frequently, pietists explain the longevity of the Torah, or the Bible in general, on the basis of its intrinsic truths. Such people relate to it as the "word of God" and the book's message is thought to be eternal by definition—that is, an eternal Being produces an eternal text. For critically minded readers, cognizant of the contemporary study of literature and culture, science and history, such an explanation proves implausible. Besides the fact that books are written by people, not gods, the very notion that the Torah contains something of divine origin or something "unique" for all humanity situates its advocates in an unwinnable contest with other cultures that make similar claims about their own literary legacies. Think of this as the literary parallel to an arms race. Christians and Muslims could easily argue that the veracity of their literature is far greater than ancient Hebrew Scriptures, a truth that is manifest in the fact that more people have adopted those religions. The only way to diffuse such arguments—by Jews, Christians, and Muslims alike—is to deny the privilege of any literature on the basis of some *intrinsic* characteristic. Why one literature or religion catches on, and another wanes, is a question for historians to debate. But intrinsic truth or "eternal" characteristics should never enter the discussion. Indeed, throughout history there have been innumerable instances of utterly ridiculous and implausible ideas winning out over far more tenable and potentially provable truths. History is as much a stage for the absurd as for the cogent.

Once this is understood, we are free to turn toward a different set of questions. What function did this book have such that it could foster a civilization faced with the adverse conditions of diaspora? Have other works in history emulated its model? Can religions today produce new literatures around which a people might rally and enhance their cultural legacy?

These essays have provided one passageway toward appreciating the real-life ideological concerns pursued by the authors of Genesis. My approach in these essays has been targeted directly at the liberal readings that do not sufficiently grapple with the notion that all literature is implicitly, if not explicitly, ideological; that all literature is dependent upon the constraints of a cultural repertoire; that no literature can be read neutrally because no literature is written neutrally. To read any part of Torah as if it were exempt from scrutiny within the ethical and social understandings of our own world is to ascribe to a biblical fundamentalism that will quickly lead to the demise of thoughtful, liberal religious perspectives. Biblical literature needs to be read creatively, ethically, *and* critically. The vibrancy of such perspectives is contingent upon the degree to which a rich, multi-faceted reading strategy can be achieved.

The life of an ancient Jewish community is what Genesis is about. The power of this book lies in its authors' conviction that a literature can create the basis for solidarity even in the face of hostile historical circumstances. At some level, the details of the stories and their ongoing relevance do not matter; rather, what matters is the *cultural vocabulary* that emerges when people share a single document as the jumping-off point for reflecting upon history, life, and their potential sources of meaning. Torah was written to create a people in an era of adversity. The fact that the "truths" of history have changed since then, that our historical condition now confronts radically different circumstances, does not diminish the potential for Torah to foster a shared experience for talking *about* history. It is through that dialogue—that grappling with text—that a common vocabulary emerges and a cultural repertoire is formed, giving rise to a collective identity and the sense of a shared destiny. Richard Rorty puts it this way: "Human solidarity is . . . a matter of sharing . . . a common selfish hope, the hope that one's world—the little things around which one has woven into one's final vocabulary—will not be destroyed." This notion of solidarity, argues Rorty, "has to be constructed out of little pieces, rather than found already waiting."[1] Genesis offers some potentially vibrant "little pieces." The reader must make of them a vocabulary for the life of an ongoing community. When that begins to take place, then "perhaps the LORD, the God of Hosts, will be gracious to the remnant of Joseph" (Amos 5:15).

1. Richard Rorty, *Contingency, Irony, and Solidarity* (Cambridge: Cambridge University Press, 1989) 92, 94.

Afterword

On Influences and Suggested Readings

The phrase "anxiety of influence" was used by Harold Bloom to suggest that a young poet is constantly struggling against the influences of a handful of literary masters.[1] Those masters cast a shadow so broad and so dark as to make the development of a unique artistic voice extremely difficult. Only what Bloom called "strong poets" manage to find a modality of expression that takes them out of that shadow; the rest labor within a prison of mediocrity.

The pejorative character of Bloom's imagery, typifying good writing as only resulting from a struggle against influences, surely describes the life of many authors—novelists, playwrights, and scholars alike. There is no question that even for doctoral students, it takes time to find one's own voice. Still, I prefer to embrace the notion of *indebtedness* with an open acknowledgement and expression of gratitude to those whose learning enhanced my own sense of the world. There can be a certain joy in discipleship, even though we must remain cognizant that eventually, we must find our own voices.

It is impossible for anyone to fully account for how teachers, colleagues, and authors-never-met, have collectively influenced how a person thinks and creates. As one spends a lifetime studying, the genealogy of ideas becomes blurred as the amount of learning increases. Even so, I shall endeavor to acknowledge those teachers and authors whose contribution to my thinking can be discerned explicitly or implicitly among the pages of this brief volume. But I shall also reference works readers might wish to consult for furthering their knowledge.

---

1. Harold Bloom, *The Anxiety of Influence* (1973).

Many things distinguish writing for a broad audience from writing for a professional audience. When writing for one's colleagues, an author can assume a high degree of background knowledge. Additionally, the style of writing can be somewhat more technical, which means that shared assumptions allow steps in an argument to be left implicit. There is scholarship, however, that someone holding a basic familiarity with a field can navigate successfully, even if it requires a bit more effort. Even this volume, targeted at a broad readership, assumes a certain familiarity with the Hebrew Bible. That is, if you grew up in a part of the world in which the Bible was unknown, this volume would not be a good first-book on the subject. Among the titles I will reference below, there are some works that squarely fall outside the genre of "popular reading," and yet, I believe that a person who has a solid familiarity with Bible will gain a great deal by considering them.

HEBREW BIBLE

My sense of the Hebrew Bible as a work of literature developed under the guidance of Mattitiahu Tsevat and subsequently Michael Fishbane. Tsevat's remarkable essays in *The Meaning of the Book of Job and Other Biblical Studies* (1980) remain important and many are accessible to a lay audience. The lead essay on Job as well as the essays on the Sabbath and the literary structure of Isaiah 6 are all very readable. Fishbane's *Biblical Interpretation in Ancient Israel* (1985) requires advanced knowledge of biblical literature, but his *Biblical Text and Texture: A Literary Reading of Selected Texts* (1998) is a book I have used successfully with undergraduates.

As for the general idea of Bible as literature, the bibliographic choices are expansive, but a few prominent works should be cited. Robert Alter's works from the 1980s, *The Art of Biblical Narrative* (1981) and *The Art of Biblical Poetry* (1985), influenced a whole generation of emerging scholars. He has since written commentaries to the Torah and a variety of literary guides and discussions of stories and characters in the so-called historiographic books. Marc Zvi Brettler has published an array of books for general audiences, which are both sophisticated and highly readable. His *How to Read the Jewish Bible* (2007) and essays on *The Book of Judges* (2002) are particularly enjoyable. I wish to acknowledge the writings of three other scholars whose influence is, in some cases directly, and in other cases, indirectly visible in this volume. The first is Norman K. Gottwald, who integrated dialectical materialism—that is, Marxist theory—into the study of ancient Israel, first in *The Tribes of Yahweh* (1979) and then in his still useful introductory textbook, *The Hebrew Bible: A Socio-literary Introduction* (1985, somewhat updated in 2009). During my graduate studies, I read avidly works by John Van Seters, starting with his *In Search of History* (1983). Regardless of whether one fully accepts his reconstruction of the literary history of Torah in its every detail, Van Seters remains an important thinker whose creativity alone is inspirational. Finally, works by E. Theodore Mullen, *Narrative History and Ethnic Boundaries* (1993) and *Ethnic Myths and Pentateuchal Foundations* (1997) are underappreciated and should find their way to more general audiences.

THE LITERATURE OF THE ANCIENT NEAR EAST

Most of us who studied Hebrew Bible as graduate students in the 1970s and 1980s were reared within a worldview that believed a key to understanding many biblical stories and law was held by Ancient Near Eastern (ANE) literature. To gain use of this key, one required extensive philological training in ancient Semitic languages, such Akkadian and Ugaritic, or some non-Semitic but regionally significant languages, such as Hittite and Sumerian. The tides were beginning to shift during the 1980s as many scholars began to relate to the Pentateuch, as well as other biblical passages, as a decidedly post-exilic document. The literatures of the Second Temple Period emerged as increasingly important, as did a variety of genres in surrounding literatures not previously thought relevant to Hebrew Bible. This shifted the emphasis from cuneiform-written languages to the alphabetic languages, especially Aramaic. Among scholars, there was something of a divide emerging between those who believed that to speak of "the Hebrew Bible in its historical context" was to speak about the Tanakh against a backdrop of Ancient Near Eastern literature, whereas others saw greater benefit in focusing on Persian and later Hellenistic era literatures. The divide, still seen among graduate programs to this day, is largely artificial. There are some things best studied with ANE literature in mind; there are other things that should be contextualized differently. Cuneiform script continued well into the Roman era as a kind of scholastic convention. Scribes living in the fourth century BCE remained aware of sources that derived from the recesses of antiquity, without, of course, being able to date them accurately.

The "origins" of a given Akkadian or Ugaritic work is less relevant than the role it may have played many centuries after it was written.

I remember reading with great excitement Thorkild Jacobsen's *The Treasures of Darkness: A History of Mesopotamian Religion* (1976) when it first appeared. Today I find many of its claims and interpretations difficult to sustain; still, it's fun readings. Jean Bottéro's *Everyday Life in Ancient Mesopotamia* (1992 in French; 2001 in English) and *The Birth of God: The Bible and the Historian* (2003) are also accessible to a general readership. The prolific David Damrosch, perhaps best known for his anthologies of world literature, penned two books relevant to the subject matter in this volume: *The Narrative Covenant: Transformations of Genre in the Growth of Biblical Literature* (1987) and subsequently, *The Buried Book: The Loss and Rediscovery of the Great Epic of Gilgamesh* (2007). Both are written from the perspective of someone immersed in comparative literature. My teacher, Tzvi Abusch, recently published *Male and Female in the Epic of Gilgamesh* (2015), a collection of essays written over many years, which expound through detailed readings the Gilgamesh story.

There is, today, a massive bibliography of works on the Ancient Near East, including Egypt, that might be cited, but I will include here just four collections of primary sources. First, there's James B. Pritchard, ed., *Ancient Near Eastern Texts Relating to the Old Testament* (3rd ed., 1969) and *The Ancient Near Eastern Pictures Relating to the Old Testament* (2nd ed., 1969). While many scholars have improved upon both the textual versions available to Pritchard and the translations in this volume, these are still valuable collections, especially because the pictures. See also William H. Hallo and Lawson Younger, eds., *The Context of* Scripture, 4 vols. (1997, 2000, 2002, and 2017), and Benjamin R. Foster, *Before the Muses: An Anthology of Akkadian Literature*, 2 vols. (3rd ed., 2005). Miriam Lichtheim published three volumes of ancient Egyptian literature: *Ancient Egyptian Literature: A Book of Readings* (1973, 1976, 1980). Two other anthologies, with very helpful introductory essays, might also be of interest: Stephanie Dalley, *Myths from Mesopotamia: Creation, the Flood, Gilgamesh and Others* (2008, rev. ed.); and Martha T. Roth, *Law Collections from Mesopotamia and Asia Minor* (1997).

POST-BIBLICAL STUDIES

Early in my studies, three professors shaped my sense of medieval Hebrew literature, history, and philology. Werner Weinberg introduced me to medieval Hebrew commentaries and the high grammarians of medieval Spain—particularly Yonah ibn Janakh and Abraham ibn Ezra. Weinberg's *Essays on Hebrew* (1993) includes a concise history of the Hebrew language and other general articles that should receive more attention among lay audiences. At the Hebrew University, I studied medieval Hebrew poetry with Dan Pagis and Ezra Fleischer. Sadly, their scholarship has not been translated into English as of this time. I recognize that my approach to both prose and poetry is heavily indebted to their classroom seminars and vast writings on the history and interpretation of Hebrew literature. Pagis and Weinberg were both survivors of Nazi concentration camps. Pagis has left us a significant body of poetry, some of which has been translated into English by Stephen Mitchell (*Variable Directions*, 1989; and *The Selected Poems of Dan Pagis*, 1996). Weinberg's *Self-portrait of a Holocaust Survivor* has been reprinted by the Hebrew Union College Press (2017). The essays in this volume are among the most sensitive and sophisticated treatments of theological and psychological aspects of survivorship ever penned.

Aspects of medieval Jewish life and history, as depicted in Hebrew literature, are exposed in Susan Einbinder's two volumes, *Beautiful Death: Jewish Poetry and Martyrdom in Medieval France* (2002) and *No Place of Rest: Jewish Literature, Expulsion, and the Memory of Medieval France* (2008). While these volumes do not present themselves as "introductions" to the field, they are extremely lucid and fascinating reconstructions of historical episodes captured in poetry.

HERMENEUTICS AND THEORY

Hermeneutics is the formal word for a *philosophy of interpretation*. As noted in the introduction to this volume, we all bring to a text attitudes as to how we will derive meaning from its content. Most of us are unable to articulate how we go about this task; it's just part of who we are as readers. But there is an entire branch of theory that investigates the *way we read and create meaning*. Today we commonly use the word "theory" to speak of reflections on the forms of knowledge conveyed in literature and historiography. I wish to discuss a handful of authors who write not about biblical studies, but about theory and philosophy. Each has profoundly influenced my sense of the world.

As a graduate student, my life was turned upside down by Michel Foucault, even though I never heard him mentioned in a single lecture by any of my professors. Foucault's important works are too numerous to cite in this context, and I readily admit that his writing is not easily navigated. But he is too important not to mention and I would urge readers to get hold of the many studies that explain his writings—they constitute a worthy and valuable shortcut to understanding an extremely complicated but influential thinker (for instance, *Understanding Foucault* [2000] by Geoff Danaher, Tony Schirato, and Jenn Webb). In an interview, the novelist Elias Khoury reminisces about attending lectures by Foucault at the Collège de France in Paris during the 1980s. "The Collège had to open several auditoriums just to fit the crowds," he recalls; "We'd arrive three or four hours early with our sandwiches and get a good seat. Foucault was like a wizard . . ." (*The Paris Review* 220 [2017] 28). When is the last time you heard of any humanities professor commanding such an audience?

Hayden White's *Metahistory: The Historical Imagination in Nineteenth-Century Europe* (1973) is among the most cited works on the philosophy of history. I am cognizant of White's contribution constantly in my own writing, and I am deeply indebted to his insights. Unfortunately, this is also an extremely difficult book, best read with the guidance of an expert.

I require of all my doctoral students to read Wolfgang Iser's *The Act of Reading: A Theory of Aesthetic Response*, first released in English in 1980. Two years later his University of Constance colleague, Hans Robert Jauss, saw his *Toward an Aesthetic of Reception* also appear in English. These are also difficult reading, but they are transformative for how one thinks about our approach to literary works.

The works of Dan Sperber and Ray Jackendoff deserve mention. Sperber is a polymath, writing about anthropology, sociology, linguistics, cognition, psychology, and often—though indirectly—religion. His 1985 work, written with Deidre Wilson, *Relevance: Communication and Cognition* is accessible as it exposes how we imbue everything from gestures to complex discourse with meaning. His recent *Enigma of Reason* (2017), written with Hugo Mercier, is highly readable. Sperber and Mercier discuss how beliefs are formed and what influences us to change our minds.

I had the privilege to study with Ray Jackendoff briefly in graduate school. Jackendoff's approach to linguistics, culture and cognition offer a radical departure from more traditional generative linguistics. Luckily, he has provided us with a number of highly readable—even entertaining—explorations of how and why human beings are generators of meaning. The most accessible is, *A User's Guide to Thought and Meaning* (2012); with a little more effort, readers will benefit greatly from, *Language, Consciousness, Culture: Essays on Mental Structure* (2007). *Foundations of Language: Brain, Meaning, Grammar, Evolution* (2003) and *Simpler Syntax* (2005), written with Peter W. Culicover, were penned for readers with extensive background in linguistics. But some of the ideas explored in these two volumes are echoed in the two books noted.

I will end by again citing Richard Rorty's *Contingency, Irony, and Solidarity* (1989), which factors into the closing sentiments of my narrative (see n25). This radical thinker will never enjoy broad influence, but few authors have written as passionately about the power of literature and its ability to bring meaning to life. After being diagnosed with cancer and knowing he had but a brief time to live, Rorty wrote the following about the importance of literature to life:

> I now wish I had spent somewhat more of my life with verse. This is not because I fear having missed out on truths that are incapable of statement in prose. There are no such truths; there is nothing about death that Swinburne and Landor knew but Epicurus and Heidegger failed to grasp. Rather, it is because I would have lived more fully if I had been able to rattle off more old chestnuts—just as I would have if I had made more close friends. Cultures with richer vocabularies are more fully human—farther removed from the beasts—than those with poorer ones; individual men and women are more fully human when their memories are amply stocked with verses.[2]

2. Richard Rorty, original published November 2007, available at the Poetry Foundation: https://www.poetryfoundation.org/poetrymagazine/articles/detail/68949.